A JOVIAL CREW

A JOVIAL CREW

by Richard Brome

Adapted by Stephen Jeffreys

WARNER CHAPPELL PLAYS

LONDON

A Time Warner Company

First published in 1992
by Warner Chappell Plays Ltd
129 Park Street, London W1Y 3FA

Copyright © 1992 by Stephen Jeffreys

ISBN 0 85676 162 1

A JOVIAL CREW was first performed by the Royal Shakespeare Company at the Swan Theatre, Stratford-upon-Avon, on 13 April, 1992, with the following cast:

SQUIRE OLDRENTS' HOUSEHOLD

OLDRENTS *a landowner*		Paul Jesson
RACHEL	} *his daughters*	Rebecca Saire
MERIEL		Emily Raymond
HILLIARD	} *their lovers*	Stephen Casey
VINCENT		Pearce Quigley
HEARTY *a gentleman*		Maxwell Hutcheon
SPRINGLOVE *a steward*		Ron Cook
RANDALL *a bailey*		David Westhead
AN USHER	*servants*	Antony Bunsee
A BUTLER	*to*	Ciaran McIntyre
A COOK	} OLDRENTS	Ian Taylor
A CHAPLAIN		James Connolly

JUSTICE CLACK'S HOUSEHOLD

JUSTICE CLACK *a magistrate*   Roger Frost
OLIVER *his son*   Dominic Mafham
AMIE *his ward*   Sophie Okonedo
TALLBOY *her suitor*   John Hodgkinson
MARTIN *a clerk*   Dorian MacDonald
SENTWELL *a captain of the watch*   John McAndrew
NUGENT *a constable*   Barnaby Kay

THE BEGGING CREW

THE PATRICO   Lloyd Hutchinson
A BEGGAR   John Hodgkinson
CECILY *a doxy*   Elizabeth Renihan
A PICKPURSE   Dorian MacDonald
A YOUNG BEGGAR   Barnaby Kay
A SLY BEGGAR   Dominic Mafham
A BEGGAR ACTOR   James Connolly
MEG *an autem mort*   Angela Vale
A BEGGAR LAWYER   Antony Bunsee

LIZ *a mort* — Emily Watson
BEN BUTLER *a pamphleteer* — Roger Frost
A BEGGAR COURTIER — Ian Taylor
A BEGGAR SOLDIER — Ciaran McIntyre
A SHORT-HAIRED BEGGAR — Jasper Britton
JOAN COPE *a vagrant* — Tracy-Ann Oberman

Director	Max Stafford-Clark
Designer	Fotini Dimou
Lighting Designer	Wayne Dowdeswell
Lyrics	Ian Dury
Music	Mickey Gallagher
Movement Director	Sue Lefton
Assistant Director	Piers Ibbotson
Stage Manager	Alison Owen
Deputy Stage Manager	Sheonagh Darby
Assistant Stage Manager	Chris Savage
Musical Director and arrangements by	Michael Tubbs

GLOSSARY

Canting, the slang language of the criminal classes, is occasionally used by the beggars in *A Jovial Crew*. Here are some key terms:

Autem	*Church*
Autem Mort	*Beggar woman married in a church*
Bing a wast	*Let's go!* or *Go away!*
Bousing ken	*Alehouse*
Caster	*Cloak*
Couch a hogshead	*Lie down and sleep*
Cuffin	*Man, bloke*
Darkmans	*Night*
Dell	*Virgin*
Doxy	*Beggar girl no longer a virgin*
Fullams	*Dice*
Frummagem	*To choke, strangle*
Gentry cove	*Nobleman*
Glaziers	*Eyes*
Harman beck	*Constable*
Jockam	*Penis*
Lap	*Milk*
Lightmans	*Day*
Mort	*Woman*
Niggle	*Have sex with*
Pannam	*Bread*
Patrico	*A hedge priest*
Pickpurse	*Pickpocket*
Prigger of prancers	*Horse thief*
Ruffin	*The Devil*
Ruffmans	*The woods, hedges and bushes*
Queer cuffin	*Justice of the peace*
Scamble	*Stumble along*
Skipper	*Barn*
Strummel	*Straw*
Whids	*Slang terms*

AUTHOR'S INTRODUCTION

Richard Brome (c.1590-1653) was one of the most popular dramatists of the period between the late 1620's and the outbreak of the Civil War. He had been servant to Ben Jonson before making a career on the stage. He wrote nineteen plays including *The City Wit* (1628), *The Northern Lass* (1629), *The Sparagus Garden* (1635), and *The Antipodes* (1638). *A Jovial Crew* (1641) is generally reckoned to be his masterpiece, but it has never gained a permanent place in the repertoire, being last publicly revived in England by Charles Lamb in 1819.

The Royal Shakespeare Company had been contemplating a production in the Swan Theatre for some time and sent the play to Max Stafford-Clark towards the end of 1991. Max responded positively but felt it would need a little re-working and recruited me for the task.

Brome's play is powered by a striking and original conceit and contains some brilliantly sustained comic scenes. It is also a fascinating social document of a precise historical period. Unfortunately it presents insuperable problems for modern directors and audiences: much of the comedy depends on contemporary references and analogies - the begging crew are an idealised literary device rather than a collection of dramatic characters; the central dramatic problem is resolved too quickly and so the second half falls apart, sustained only by a series of running gags; the denouement is wildly implausible and contradicts much of the psychology of the central character, Springlove.

I spoke to a number of people who had attended a workshop production of the original text in the National Theatre's studio, and the overall impression was that the play as it stood was unperformable. I then read Martin Butler's excellent book Theatre and Crisis, 1632-1642 which argues persuasively that *A Jovial Crew,* far from being an escapist romp, is a 'state of the nation' play set at a moment of decisive political transformation. My aim was to deliver this hidden play from the conventions and codes of the period and to make Brome's comic conception work on stage. At the end of the process, the RSC's literary department counted the lines and told me I had written 45 per cent of the final text. Here is a brief outline of who wrote what:

SCENE ONE: I show the Patrico making the prophecy which initiates the plot. In Brome, it is reported in a scene between Oldrents and Hearty.

SCENE TWO: I re-wrote most of the beggar's speeches with the aim giving the crew a more realistic social background.

SCENE THREE: This is virtually the scene Brome wrote, but with some new comic additions.

SCENE FOUR: This scene is completely my own invention. It tries to show the reality of the begging life and establishes Brome's splendid creation of Justice Clack.

SCENE FIVE: I added Hearty's speech on carving terms.

SCENE SIX: Brome calls for a dance without giving any indication of what its effect should be. There were ecstatic dancing cults a few years later, and we decided to use this moment to suggest some of the turmoil which was soon to follow.

SCENE SEVEN: This is the scene Brome wrote with a little re-arranging and some new gags.

SCENE EIGHT: Like Scene Four, this is wholly my invention. In Brome, Amie and Springlove meet and decide to marry without spending any time together. I felt this scene was necessary in order for the audience to believe in Springlove's final abandonment of the begging life.

SCENE NINE: I changed Oldrents' motivation for going to Justice Clack's.

SCENE TEN: I have extended and widened the beggars' discussion of what play to perform.

SCENE ELEVEN: I added this short scene to show the amateur beggars (except Meriel) suffering from the hardships of the begging life.

SCENE TWELVE: Brome's play within a play merely recapitulates the plot of *A Jovial Crew*. It's curious that he should have abandoned the idea of a play about Utopia after carefully planting it in Scene Ten. Perhaps he simply ran out of steam or perhaps the political situation was too unstable for this kind of presentation to take place. At any rate, I followed through Brome's original notion, using the form of the Mumming play. I also simplified the Patrico's revelation and introduced the defection of Meriel and a section of the crew at the very end, suggesting, I hope, the imminent fissure in English society.

Randall's first monologue is close to Brome's original; the rest are my inventions.

I must thank the acting company who threw themselves into the production with great trust, energy and skill; to Ian Dury whose hoary cast and command of canting would have earned him a slot in any seventeenth century crew; to Mickey Gallagher whose wonderful music is included here; to Fotini Dimou who was an inspired collaborator; to Sue Lefton and Piers Ibbotson who kept on coming up with ideas; and to a wonderful stage management team who were the most visible manifestation of the RSC's excellent support. Mostly I must thank Max Stafford-Clark for inviting me to participate in a fascinating and unusual project and for sustaining me during its completion.

Stephen Jeffreys

PROLOGUE

The overture plays. A Beggar *comes on. He removes his cap.*

BEGGAR   The title of our play *A Jovial Crew*
                 May seem to promise mirth, which were a
                                                     new
                 And forc'd thing in these sad and tragic days
                 For you to find or we express in plays.
                 We wish you then would change that
                                               expectation,
                 Since jovial mirth is now grown out of
                                                   fashion.
                 Strife, private and public, holds the stage
                 Aping the civil quarrels of our age;
                 And those gallants who comic fare demand,
                 Like beggars with an empty outstretched hand
                 Sit hungry midst the clash of sword and drum,
                 Awaiting sustenance that never comes.
                 Still at our play we hope you may feast long;
                 On wit, device, dance, argument and song.
                 But yet I know not if 'twill please you well
                 Our future, unlike some, I can't foretell.

                 (*The* BEGGAR *indicates the* PATRICO *who has
                 come on with* OLDRENTS, *then exits.*)

ACT ONE

SCENE ONE

A room in OLDRENTS' *house.* PATRICO *is reading* OLDRENTS'
hand.

PATRICO   And to the farming of your lands, sir,
                 I see your fortune flourishes apace:
                 Grain will yield well and cattle chew the cud
                 Fattening themselves to fill the peoples'
                                                     trenchers.

OLDRENTS   But which will profit better, crop or beast?

PATRICO   Both will hold their price, but see: here runs
                   A line to Mercury (that's the little finger)
                   Which speaks of blood and money in an
                                                    instant:
                   The price of meat will rise much faster than
                   The price of corn.

                   (RANDALL *comes on, places a drink for the*
                   PATRICO *on the table, then goes out.*)

OLDRENTS   I'll turn my sixty acres
                   By the top road out to pasture. But to
                   My daughters and my household: prophesy.

PATRICO   Your household, sir, no finer nor more trusty
                   Band of servants lives. The love they bear
                   For you surpasses all description and
                   Your tenants will respect the tithes and duties
                   Owed you for as long as I can see.

OLDRENTS   What necromancy's this that can discern
                   The price of wheat and livestock, but baulks
                   To speak of kith and kin. What of my
                   daughters?

PATRICO   Sir, these are uncertain times: King
                   And Commons clutch at one others' throats,
                   The parson preaches 'gainst his flock, men
                                                    starve.
                   The end of the world is whisper'd high and
                                                    low.
                   Delight in your happy palm and do not seek
                   To peer too far behind the covering cloud.

OLDRENTS   I know there's more to this: speak of my
                                                    daughters.

PATRICO   I see their future but I dread to speak.

OLDRENTS   Then put your qualms behind you: for Truth
                                                    I'll pay.
                   I will not hang the bearer of bad news.

PATRICO   Then bend yourself unto the worst. These
Lines here at the base of Mercury
Are your two daughters fair. They commence
                      well
But then they turn away to mean insolvency.

OLDRENTS   I still crave more:

PATRICO   Then ask these cards to speak:

(*The* PATRICO *fans a pack of cards, offering
them to* OLDRENTS *who picks three cards and
places them face down on the table. The*
PATRICO *then reveals them in turn.*)

One for the past, one for the present and one
For what's to come. Here's the past: the
                    Lovers -
Marriage, happiness: and here's our present
                    plight
The Wheel of Fortune's upside down: now
                    look
What comes, the Hermit in his mean brown
                    habit.
These cards shape pictures in the mind which
I must own to. I see your daughters clad
In beggars' rags.

OLDRENTS   In truth?

PATRICO   Upon my life.

OLDRENTS   Go. Here's money. No. Take more. I'll not
Insult the chiromancer's art.

PATRICO   Master.

(OLDRENTS *turns away.* PATRICO *drinks during*
OLDRENTS' *speech, then goes.*)

OLDRENTS   This above all things I have fear'd. Lands
Have I bought and sold, crops sown and
                    harvested,
Streams diverted and barren fields made
                    green.

I have march'd teams of men to war at
                     Nature:
And to what end? To keep us all in comfort
From the wind and rain, but most my
                     daughters:
The treasures of my heart whom now I find
Will wander destitute amongst the poor.
Oh curse upon all superstitious minds
That meddle, then recoil from what they find.

(*Enter* HEARTY.)

HEARTY

What Oldrents? Loitering here when we could
Be making horseback expedition
Or glowing o'er our sack and song.

OLDRENTS

I pray you, Hearty, do not speak. I am
Bereft of cheer, that was so full of joy
But ten minutes past.

HEARTY

                What news has struck you thus?

OLDRENTS

News? No. I am plagu'd by tales of what's
To come, not what has passed.

HEARTY

                Oldrents. You have
Not once again returned to that pernicious
Vice of prophecy.

OLDRENTS

                I fear I have:
And it has proved most lamentable to
My hopes. One among the beggar crew
Who visit us tonight possesses a most
Cunning knowledge of what lies ahead
Through scanning of the lines upon the hand.
This Patrico (for so he calls himself)
Did scrutinise the mapwork of my palm
And therein saw the vision (God protect me
From't) of my two daughters destitute
And begging for their provender in rags.

HEARTY

And this is all your cause of gloom. You
Appear as one whose ship of life is dash'd
Upon a fatal rock by this slight breeze.

OLDRENTS   It has indeed, friend, much afflicted me.

HEARTY   And very justly, let me tell you, sir,
            That could so impiously be curious
            To tempt a judgement on you, to give ear,
            And faith too (by your leave) to fortune-
                                            tellers,
            Wizards and gypsies!

OLDRENTS   And now will I be frighted
            With't in a thousand dreams.

HEARTY   I would be drunk
            A thousand times to bed, rather than dream
            Of any of their riddlemy riddlemies.
            Trust 'em? Hang 'em! Old blind buzzards!
            For once they hit, they miss a thousand times;
            And most times give quite contrary, bad for
                                            good,
            And best for worst. One told a gentleman
            His son should be a man killer and hang'd
                                            for't:
            Who after proved a great and rich physician,
            And with fame i' the university
            Was hang'd up in picture for a grave example.
            That was the whim of that. Quite contrary!

OLDRENTS   And that was happy; would mine could so
                                        deceive my fears.

HEARTY   Now I come to you: your figure-flinger finds
            That both your daughters, notwithstanding all
            Your great possessions, which they are coheirs
                                            of,
            Shall yet be beggars. May it not be meant
            They may prove courtiers, or great courtiers'
                                            wives,
            And so be beggars in law? Is not that
            The whim on't, think you? You shall think no
                                        worse on't.

OLDRENTS   Would I had your merry heart.

HEARTY   I thank you, sir.

OLDRENTS   I mean the like.

HEARTY   I would you had; and I
Such an estate as yours. Four thousand yearly,
With such a heart as mine, would defy fortune
And all her babbling soothsayers.
Think like a man of conscience (now I am
                                        serious).
What justice can there be for such a curse?
Are you not the only rich man lives unenvied?
Have you one grudging tenant? Do they not
                                        make
Their children pray for you morn and evening
                                        as
Duly as for King and Realm? Will they
Not all fight for you?

OLDRENTS   It is their natural goodness.

HEARTY   It is your merit. Your great love and bounty
Procures from Heaven those inspirations in 'em.
Whose rent did ever you exact? Whose have
You not remitted, when by casualties
Of fire, of floods, of common dearth, or
                                        sickness,
Poor men were brought behindhand?

OLDRENTS   Enough, good friend, no more.

HEARTY   These are enough, indeed,
To fill your ears with joyful acclamations
Where'er you pass: "Heaven bless our
                              Landlord Oldrents,
Our Master Oldrents, our good Patron
                              Oldrents."
Cannot these sounds conjur this evil spirit
Of fear out of you? Shall Squire Oldrents'
                              daughters
Wear old rents in their garments (there's a
                              whim too)
Because a fortune teller told you so?

(*Enter* SPRINGLOVE *with books and papers; he
lays them on the table.*)

OLDRENTS   Come, I will strive to think no more on't.

HEARTY   Will you ride forth for air then, and be merry?

OLDRENTS   Your counsel and example may instruct me.

HEARTY   Sack must be had in sundry places too
                For songs I am provided.

OLDRENTS   Yet here comes one brings me a second fear,
                Who has my care the next unto my children.

HEARTY   Your steward, sir, it seems has business with
                                                            you.
                I wish you would have none.

OLDRENTS   I'll soon dispatch it,
                And then be for our journey instantly.

HEARTY   I'll wait your coming down, sir.

                (*Exit* HEARTY.)

OLDRENTS   But why, Springlove,
                Is now this expedition?

SPRINGLOVE   Sir, 'tis duty.

OLDRENTS   'Tis duty to complete our half year's accounts
                By the fifth of May, which date yet stands
                                                  some ten days
                Off. It is not common among stewards
                To urge in their accounts before the day
                Their lords have limited.

SPRINGLOVE   Sir, I trust you do not chide me for too swift
                Completion of my labours?

OLDRENTS   Springlove, I chide
                You in nothing. You are a steward nonpareil.

SPRINGLOVE   Your indulgence I hope shall ne'er corrupt me.

                (SPRINGLOVE *turns over the several books to
                his master.*)

Here, in these accounts, you may be pleas'd
To take full survey of all your rents
Receiv'd, and all such other payments as
Came to my hands since my last audit, for
Cattle, wool, corn, all fruits of husbandry.
Then my receipts on bonds and some new
                                        leases,
With some old debts, and almost desperate
                                        ones,
From country cavaliers as well as courtiers -
(Such men who, reckless of their estates,
                                        planted
No seedcorn in the fatter years and now
In these lean times gaze upon empty pantries.)
Then here, sir, are my several disbursements
In all particulars for yourself and daughters,
In charge of housekeeping, buildings and
                                        repairs;
Journeys, apparel, coaches, gifts and all
Expenses from your personal necessaries.
Here, servants' wages, liveries and cures,
Here for supplies of horses, hawks and
                                        hounds.
And lastly, not the least to be remember'd,
Your large benevolences to the poor.

OLDRENTS   Thy charity there goes hand in hand with
                                        mine.
              And, Springlove, I commend it in thee, that
              So humbly born art grown so high in
                                        goodness.

SPRINGLOVE   Now here, sir, is
              The balance of the several accounts,
              Which shows you what remains in cash: which
                                        added
              Unto your former bank, makes up in all -

OLDRENTS   Twelve thousand and odd pounds.

SPRINGLOVE   Here are the keys
              Of all. The chests are safe in your own closet.

OLDRENTS   Why in my closet? Is not yours as safe?

SPRINGLOVE   Oh, sir, you know my suit.

OLDRENTS   Your suit? What suit?

SPRINGLOVE   Touching the time of year.

OLDRENTS   'Tis well nigh May.
                    Why what of that, good Springlove?

SPRINGLOVE   You know, sir. I am called.

OLDRENTS   Fie, Springlove, fie.
                    I hop'd thou had abjur'd that uncouth
                                              practice.

SPRINGLOVE   You thought I had forsaken nature then.

OLDRENTS   Is that disease of nature still in thee
                    So virulent?
                    Have I first bred thee, and then preferr'd thee
                                              (from
                    I will not say how wretched a beginning)
                    To be a master over all my servants,
                    And canst thou,
                    There, slight me for the whistlings of the
                                              birds.

SPRINGLOVE   Your reason, sir, informs you that's no cause.
                    But 'tis the season of the year that calls me.
                    What moves her notes provokes my disposition
                    By a more absolute power of nature than
                    Philosophy can render an account for.

OLDRENTS   I find there's no expelling it. Still
                    It will return. I have tried all the means
                    (As I may safely think) in human wisdom,
                    And did (as near as reason could) assure me,
                    That thy last year's restraint had stopp'd
                                              forever
                    That running sore on thee, that gadding
                                              humour;
                    When, only for that cause, I laid the weight
                    Of mine estate in stewardship upon thee,
                    Which kept thee in that year, after so many
                    Summer vagaries thou hadst made before.

SPRINGLOVE   You kept a swallow on a cage that while.
              I cannot, sir, endure another summer
              In that restraint, with life; 'twas then my
                                            torment,
              But now would be my death. My life is yours,
              Who are my patron; freely may you take it.
              Yet pardon, sir, my frailty, that do beg
              A small continuance of it on my knees.

OLDRENTS   Can there no means be found to preserve life
              In thee but wand'ring like a vagabond?
              Does not the sun as comfortably shine
              Upon my gardens as the opener fields?
              Are not my walks and greens as delectable
              As the highways and commons? Are the
                                            shades
              Of sycamore and bowers of eglantine
              Less pleasing than of bramble or thorn
                                            hedges?
              Do not the birds sing here as sweet and lively
              As any other where? Is not thy bed more soft,
              And rest more safe, than in a field or barn?

SPRINGLOVE   Yea, in the winter season, when the fire
              Is sweeter than the air.

OLDRENTS   What air is wanting?

SPRINGLOVE   Oh sir, y'have heard of pilgrimages, and
              The voluntary travels of good men.

OLDRENTS   For penance, or to holy ends? But bring
              Not those into comparison, I charge you.

SPRINGLOVE   I do not, sir. But pardon me to think
              Their sufferings are much sweeten'd by
                                            delights,
              Such as we find by shifting place and air.

OLDRENTS   Are there delights in beggary? Or, if to take
              Diversity of air be such a solace,
              Travel the kingdom over; and if this
              Yield not variety enough, try further,
              Provided your deportment be gentle.

                    Take horse and man and money, I'll give you
                                                                all.

SPRINGLOVE   Dear sir, retort me naked to the world
                    Rather than lay those burdens on me which
                    Will stifle me. I must abroad or perish.
                    Now, sir, do I have your leave to go?

OLDRENTS   I leave you to dispute it with yourself
                    I have no voice to bid you go or stay;
                    My love shall give thy will pre-eminence,
                    And leave th'effect to time and providence.

                    (*Exit* OLDRENTS.)

SPRINGLOVE   I am confounded in my obligation
                    To this good man: his virtue is my
                                                        punishment,
                    When 'tis not in my nature to return
                    Obedience to his merits. I could wish
                    Such an ingratitude were death by th' law,
                    And put in present execution upon me
                    To rid me of my sharper suffering.
                    Nor but by death can this predominant sway
                    Of nature be extinguish'd in me. I
                    Have fought with my affections to conquer
                    This inborn strong desire of liberty
                    Which he detests as shameful. But I find
                    The war is endless and I needs must fly.
                    What must I lose then? A good master's love.
                    What loss feels he that wants not what he
                                                            loses?
                    They'll say I lose all reputation.
                    What's that, when living where such thing's
                                                        unknown?
                    Among the beggar crew, each man's his own.

                    (*Enter* RANDALL.)

                    Now, fellow, what news from whence you
                    came?

RANDALL   The old wonted news, sir, from your
                    guesthouse, the old barn. We have unloaden

the breadbasket, the beef kettle and the beer
bumbards there amongst your guests the
beggars. And they have all prayed for you and
our master, as their manner is, from the teeth
outward.

(*He gives an insincere smile.*)

From the teeth inwards, there is such a deal of
chomping and swallowing as to leave no
energy to expend on prayer. Save for the
belch, sir, which is a kind of prayer among
those peoples which say grace after food. Sir.

SPRINGLOVE   Thou should'st not think uncharitably.

RANDALL   Thought's free, Master Steward. But your
              charity is nonetheless notorious.

SPRINGLOVE   But Randall, charity seeks no merits nor
              popular than⊡s; 'tis well if I do well in it.

RANDALL   It might be better though (if old Randall,
              whom you allow to talk might counsel) to
              help breed up poor men's children; or decayed
              labourers past their work; or towards the
              setting up of poor, young married couples
              than to bestow an hundred pound a year,
              besides your master's bounty, to maintain in
              begging such wanderers as these, that never
              are out of the way; that cannot give account
              from whence they came or whither they go;
              nor of any beginning they had, or any end
              they seek, but still to stroll and beg till their
              bellies be full and then sleep till they be
              hungry.

SPRINGLOVE   Thou art ever repining at those poor people!
              They take nothing from thee but thy pains,
              and that I pay thee for. Why should'st thou
              grudge?

RANDALL   Am I not bitten every day by the lice they
              leave in their litter? Lice? Six foot

bloodhounds, sir. When a beggar crew is in our barn, I am a walking charity to every insect in Nottinghamshire. Daily I do lose more blood than ever was shed by my great grandsire at Agincourt.

SPRINGLOVE   Come, come, our hospitality is but for a night. Your begging crew will always move onward in the morning.

RANDALL   To be replaced by fresher vagrants. We daily change one rabble for another as they do collars in the court.

SPRINGLOVE   Thou art old Randall still, ever grumbling. But you have had merry blasts with some of 'em!

RANDALL   I am not much for merriment myself, Master Steward. I lack the capering spirit, though I am content to observe it in others, once a sixmonth or so.

SPRINGLOVE   Well, honest Randall, thus it is. I am for a journey. I know not how long will be my absence, but I will presently take order with the cook, pantler and butler for my wonted allowance to the poor; and I will leave money with thee to manage the affair till my return.

RANDALL   I am to be the bailiff of your beggars?

SPRINGLOVE   Even so.

RANDALL   Lord, how a man can rise i' the world. And it not yet eleven i' the morning.

SPRINGLOVE   Well, well. We will agree upon't anon. Bustle now about your business.

RANDALL   Bustle sir? No, not I. I am more your lingerer than your bustler. In a house such as this sir, your bustler is too great a disturber of dust. Bailiff of beggary!

(*Exit* RANDALL.)

SPRINGLOVE   I cannot think but with a trembling fear
On this adventure, in a scruple which
I have not weighed with all my other doubts.
I shall in my departure rob my master.
Of what? Of a true servant; other theft
I have committed none. And that may be
                      supplied,
And better, too, by some more constant to
                      him.
But I may injure many in his trust,
Which now he cannot but be sparing of.
I rob him too of the content and hopes
He had in me, whom he had built and rais'd
Unto that growth in his affection
That I became a gladness in his eye,
And now must be a grief or a vexation . . .

(*We hear a beggarwoman -* MEG *- singing
during* SPRINGLOVE'S *speech, 'Born to the
Life'.*)

MEG   Harsh hunger is rife, I was born to the life,
For I am a vagabond's daughter;
Shall I sleep in a bed, or my belly be fed . . .

SPRINGLOVE   . . . Unto his noble heart. But hark! Ay, there's
The harmony that drowns all doubts and fears.

ALL   . . . When hens make holy water!

SPRINGLOVE   The emperor hears no such music, nor feels
content like this!

(*The* PATRICO *comes on, leading the* CREW OF
BEGGARS.)

PATRICO   A poke full of plums, a garnish of thrums
And a muck-hill on my trencher;
Are you there with your bears, shall I whistle
                    my prayers?
Or damned be this adventure.

SCENE TWO

Beggars

The BEGGARS *greet* SPRINGLOVE. *Four or five know him of old and rush towards him. Others hang back.*

1ST BEGGAR   Our master, our master!

2ND BEGGAR   Our sweet and comfortable master!

3RD BEGGAR   More than master, this is our king.

SPRINGLOVE   How cheer my hearts?

PATRICO   Excellent well, your majesty. Music! Music!

ALL   (*singing, 'The Canters are Coming'*)
                  So! Throw a good scruff to the singers and
                                                    dancers;
                  Rufflers, runagates, priggers of prancers;
                  Throw us white money whenever we ask it;
                  Doxies, dells and bawdy baskets.

                  Trouble thee not thy bodkin stranger;
                  Our entertainments hold no danger.
                  Go shoe the goose and saddle the sow
                  For the canters are coming amongst you now.

                  The bold harman-beck may offer no charm
                  But stretching our necks as long as his arm;
                  Though pannum may stale and lap might
                                                    curdle
                  Nary an 'M' lies under our girdle.

                  Hoary of cast and weathered of caster
                  Slave to none and no-one's master,
                  Well-versed in the whids of the ruffian's art:
                  Gip! quoth Gilbert when his mare doth fart.

                  (SPRINGLOVE *is elevated onto a chair placed up
                  on the table and an improvised crown is
                  placed on his head.*)

4TH BEGGAR	Now you are crowned our king!
1ST BEGGAR	And with more right than he who squats the golden chair in London.
3RD BEGGAR	Though he be more beggar king than you!
SPRINGLOVE	Sir Patrico, this is well performed.
PATRICO	'Tis well if it like you, master. Now shall I introduce you to the newer members of our crew, that you may have familiarity of all.
ACTOR	Command us and employ us, we beseech you.
SPRINGLOVE	Thou speak'st most courtly.
ACTOR	Sir, I was an actor in London, but being within reach of the lash for playing libellous plays at London, was fain to fly into this covey and I now live very civilly and gently among the crew.
SPRINGLOVE	And do your old skills go well in your new occupation?
ACTOR	Faith sir, they stand the test. For what is beggary but a kind of play, acted out as follows: "Sir, I am hungry. If you do but press a shilling into my palm I shall eat tonight and God will save you."
SPRINGLOVE	Most excellently done.
ACTOR	You see, master, I must convince my public. Do they believe I am hungry? They do. Do they think I will spend my shilling upon victuals and not on whores and sack? They do. Do they believe that for a shilling they will go to heaven? Oh, they do, they do sir.
SPRINGLOVE	Excellent fellow, you shall have more than a shilling. (*Gives him money.*)

ACTOR	Bless you, master. I have it mind to revive my Tamburlaine with this crew in support.
BEGGAR	I'll bear you up.
ACTOR	I'm sure I can offer you a most choice line of parts.
	(*He goes off. In turn, the new members of the crew are introduced by the* PATRICO *to* SPRINGLOVE *and receive money from him.*)
PATRICO	Meg O'Malley, Master.
MEG	I was an apple woman but that's long past with the apples not being as they were and fewer and so withered and pinched like you were setting your teeth in Satan's gob and turning your stomach if you did chew and swallow, so the apples were all done-finished for me. I walked thirty mile one day and forty mile the next on two pieces of barley bread and I fell down on the road and my head was bad but I was took in by this crew and slept in a barn that night and a barn the next and that's me ever since.
PATRICO	Now a man of great skill i' the quarrel.
MEG	Thank you, sir.
LAWYER	Sir, our Patrico being a hedge priest, I am, as you might say, hedge lawyer and attorney to our crew.
SPRINGLOVE	Then I'll be no hedge king for fear thou'll impeach me for the imposing of ship money.
	(SPRINGLOVE *removes his crown and dismounts from the throne.*)
	How came you to this calling, sir?

LAWYER

By begging three years outside the law courts, your highness. Where I did begin to learn the attorney's tongue much as a dog can thrive on scraps thrown away i' the gutter. For I can strike you hard with a malice prepense or go lightly with my nolle prosequi: I can, all in an instant, deem you ultra vires and make your quietus with a mens rea. And yet, I was never at school in my life, 'tis all but air and echoes. But if you would have my prove the moon made o' blue cheese, I can do it, sir, if you do but pay me fifteen guineas an hour.

SPRINGLOVE

Well argued, attorney, here's your fee.

PATRICO

And here is Liz, a mort of the company.

LIZ

I was wife of a stonemason in London that did earn two and sixpence a day but was crushed under a stone faulty laid by his apprentice. And but two months after that I was reduc'd to nothing . . .

1ST BEGGAR

This tale was writ by the Queen o' the Fairies -

LIZ

. . . and no means of earning my living but the road and I am no longer ashamed of it, for this is what I must do and the crew is a jolly crew and does share all things alike.

2ND BEGGAR

'Tis so.

LIZ

So as you would pity your own widow that may one day be, pity me.

SPRINGLOVE

You have found good company.

LIZ

As I may be saved I think I have.

SPRINGLOVE

Old Ben Butler, you are no new man to the crew.

BEN

No, but I am a new man since I found my mystery. For I am ever busy with the printing

and selling of pamphlets. For there are many
that do wish to have their thoughts set down
and I do set them, then make a circuit
roundabouts with the crew and take money for
them. And to those that have no money, I give
them scot free in hope that they may someday
learn to read and read to learn.

SPRINGLOVE   Well, I shall buy and profit from your work.

BEN   God b'w'you, sir.

PATRICO   Here's one that cut a fine figure i' the court.

COURTIER   Sir, my father was great i' the court and
taught me as a boy the nine degrees of
bowing: first the shifting o' the eyebrows,
then the inclination of the head, the lowering
of the neck, the measured bend (that's for
your foreign diplomats), the deep bend, the
deep bend with partial arm flourish for your
privy councillor, the stoop, the stoop with
arm and hat flourish and the full grovel, the
last to be used only for monarchs. But alas I
allied myself with the wrong faction and
compounded my sin with a deep bend to a
bishop who was worthy of a stoop. 'Twas a
choice between a poignard i' the back or
flight so I now practise my obeisance on the
nation's highways and bend for a butcher as
easy as for a baron. Sir.

(*He bows.*)

SPRINGLOVE   Well bowed, sir courtier.

PATRICO   And now our warrior.

SOLDIER   Sir, I bore the name of a Netherland soldier
till I ran away from my colours. I scambled
into this country where I snapp'd up my living
in the city by my wit in cheating, pimping and
such like arts till the cart and the pillory
showed me publicly to the world. Soldiering

being the second last refuge, I enlisted 'gainst
the Scots where I amused myself on a
Saturday night by removing altar rails from
the churches; but the war being killed off
before I was dispatch'd myself, I was left
with no refuge but the last, I mean, sir,
beggary, and now in this army I am a proud
infantryman.

(*The* SHORT-HAIRED BEGGAR *comes forward. He
is an intense Puritan.*)

SHORT-HAIRED BEGGAR	I'll not call you master for I am a masterless man, save that I have a master in God. Thank you.
BEN	Well spoken.
PATRICO	What say, sir, to our crew? Are we not well congregated?
SPRINGLOVE	You are a jovial crew, the only people Whose happiness I admire.
SOLDIER	Will you make us happy serving under you? Have you any enemies? Shall we fight under you? Will you be our captain?
4TH BEGGAR	Nay our king.
SOLDIER	Command us something, sir.
SPRINGLOVE	Where's the next rendezvous?
PATRICO	Neither in village nor in town But three mile off at Mapledown.
SPRINGLOVE	Tomorrow evening there I'll visit you. Tonight I am for my own jaunt.
PREGNANT BEGGAR	I'll sing you an air of a life without care, Where a spirit could never be brisker; When fortune was true and never turned blue,
ALL	The mother of that was a whisker.

(*The* CREW *start to move off.*)

A BEGGAR   There's a chill on the heath that has frozen
                                      my teeth
              Thy servant hast thou foresaken
              Where comfort is sparse and so is mine arse.

ALL   (*off*) My voice can still beg bacon.

SPRINGLOVE   So, now away.
              They dream of happiness that live in state,
              But they enjoy it that obey their fate.

              Blackout

                        SCENE THREE

Enter VINCENT, HILLIARD, MERIEL *and* RACHEL.

VINCENT   I am overcome with admiration at the felicity
              they take!

HILLIARD   Beggars! They are the only people can boast
              the benefit of a free state, in the full
              enjoyment of liberty, mirth and ease, having
              all things in common and nothing wanting of
              nature's whole provision within the reach of
              their desires. Who would have lost this sight
              of their revels?

VINCENT   How think you, ladies? Are they not the only
              happy in a nation?

MERIEL   Happier than we, I'm sure, that are pent up
              and tied by the nose to the continual steam of
              hot hospitality here in our father's house,
              when they have the air at pleasure in all
              variety.

RACHEL   And though I know we have merrier spirits
              than they, yet to live thus confin'd stifles us.

HILLIARD   Why ladies, you have liberty enough, or may
              take what you please.

MERIEL   Yes, in our father's rule and government, or
              by his allowance. What's that to absolute
              freedom, such as the very beggars have, to
              feast and revel here today, and yonder
              tomorrow, next day where they please, and so
              on still, the whole country or kingdom over?
              There's liberty! The birds of the air can take
              no more.

RACHEL   And now today our father is so pensive (what
              muddy spirit soe'er possesses him, would I
              could conjure't out) that he makes us even
              sick of his sadness. We, that were wont to see
              my gossip's cock today, mold cocklebread,
              dance clutterdepouch, and hannykin booby,
              bind barrels, or do anything before him and he
              would laugh at us.

MERIEL   Now he never looks upon us but with a sigh,
              or tears in his eyes, tho' we simper never so
              sanctifiedly. What tales have been told him of
              us, or what he suspects, I know not; God
              forgive him, I do; but I am weary of his
              house.

RACHEL   Does he think us whores, trow, because
              sometimes we talk as lightly as great ladies. I
              can swear safely for the virginity of one of us,
              so far as word and deed goes: marry,
              thought's free.

MERIEL   Which is that one of us, I pray? Yourself or
              me?

RACHEL   Good sister Meriel, charity begins at home.
              But I'll swear I think as charitably of thee,
              and not only because thou art a year younger
              neither.

MERIEL   I am beholden to you. But for my father, I
              would I knew his grief and how to cure him,

or that we were where we could not see it. It
spoils our mirth, and that has been better than
his meat to us.

VINCENT   Will you hear our motion, ladies?

MERIEL   Psew, you would marry us presently out of his
way, because he has given you a foolish kind
of promise. But we will see him in a better
humour first, and as apt to laugh as we to lie
down.

HILLIARD   'Tis like that course will cure him would you
embrace it.

RACHEL   We will have him cured first, I tell you; and
you shall wait that season and our leisure.

MERIEL   I will rather hazard my being one of the
devil's ape leaders than to marry while he is
melancholy.

RACHEL   Or I to stay in his house to give entertainment
to this knight or t'other coxcomb that comes
to cheer him up with eating of his cheer.

MERIEL   When we must fetch 'em sweetmeats -

RACHEL   - and they must tell us, "Ladies, your lips are
sweeter", and then fall into courtship, one in
a set speech taken out of old Breton's works -

MERIEL   'The Arbor of Amorous Devices', wherein
young Gentlemen may read many pleasant
fancies -

RACHEL   - another with verses out of 'The Academy of
Compliments' -

MERIEL   And then to be kiss'd, fagh!

RACHEL   And sometimes slaver'd, faughh!

MERIEL	'Tis not to be endur'd. We must out of the house. We cannot live but by laughing, and that aloud, and nobody sad within hearing.
VINCENT	We are for any adventure with you, ladies. Shall we project a journey for you? Your father has trusted you, and will think you safe in our company: and we would fain be abroad upon some progress with you. Shall we make a fling to London, and see how the spring appears there in the Spring Garden; and in Hyde Park, to see the races, horse and foot; to hear the jockeys crack and see the Adamites run naked afore the ladies?
RACHEL	We saw all that last year.
HILLIARD	But there ha' been new plays since.
VINCENT	Beeston's Boys in 'The Swaggering Damsel' -
RACHEL	No, no, no. We are not for London.
HILLIARD	What think you of a journey to the Bath then?
RACHEL	Worse than t'other way. I love not to carry my health where others drop their diseases. There's no sport i' that.
VINCENT	Will you up to the hill top of sports, then, the Cotswold Games?
MERIEL	What? Stand i' the drizzle to watch twelve shepherds leaping a five bar gate?
RACHEL	Besides, that will be too public for our recreation. We would have it more within ourselves.
HILLIARD	Think of some course yourselves then. We are for you upon any way, as far as horse and money can carry us.
VINCENT	Ay, and if those means fail us, as far as our legs can bear, or our hands can help us.

RACHEL   And we will put you to't. (*Aside*.) Come
                aside, Meriel.

VINCENT   Some jeer, perhaps, to put upon us.

HILLIARD   What think you of a pilgrimage to Saint
                Winnifred's Well ?

VINCENT   Or a journey to the wise woman at Nantwich,
                to ask if we be fit husbands for them.

HILLIARD   They are not scrupulous in that, we having
                had their growing loves up from our
                childhoods and the old squire's good will
                before all men.

                (RACHEL *and* MERIEL *laugh aside*.)

VINCENT   What's the conceit, I marvel?

HILLIARD   Some merry one it seems.

RACHEL   And then, sirrah Meriel - hark again - ha, ha,
                ha -

VINCENT   How they are taken with it.

MERIEL   Ha, ha, ha - hark again, Rachel.

VINCENT   If it be not some trick upon us which they'll
                discover in some monstrous shape, they cozen
                me. Now, ladies, is your project ripe? Possess
                us with the knowledge of it.

RACHEL   It is more precious than to be imparted upon a
                slight demand.

HILLIARD   Pray let us hear it. You know we are your
                trusty servants.

VINCENT   And have kept all your counsels ever since we
                have been infant playfellows.

RACHEL   Yes, you have played all kinds of small game
                with us, but this is to the purpose.

HILLIARD	It seems so by their laughing.
RACHEL	And asks a stronger tongue-tie than tearing of books, burning of samplers, making dirt pies or piss and paddle in't.
VINCENT	You know how, and what we have vow'd: to wait upon you any way, any how and any whither.
MERIEL	And you will stand to't?
HILLIARD	Ay, and go to't with you, wherever it be.
	(RACHEL *and* MERIEL *cannot speak for laughing*.)
RACHEL	Pray tell 'em sister Meriel.
MERIEL	You are the elder. Pray tell it you.
RACHEL	You are the younger. I command you tell it. Come out with it, they long to have it.
MERIEL	In troth you must tell it, sister; I cannot.
RACHEL	Then, gentlemen, stand your ground.
VINCENT	Some terrible business, sure!
RACHEL	You seem'd e'en now to admire the felicity of beggars-
MERIEL	And have engag'd yourselves to join with us in any course.
RACHEL	Will you now with us, and for our sakes turn beggars? But for a time and a short progress.
MERIEL	And for a spring-trick of youth, now, in the season.
VINCENT	Beggars! What rogues are these?
HILLIARD	A simple trial of our loves and service!

RACHEL   Are you resolv'd upon't? If not, God b'w'y'.
             We are resolved to take our course.

MERIEL   Let yours be to keep counsel.

             (*They make as if to go.*)

VINCENT   Stay, stay. Beggars! Are we not so already?
             Do we not beg your loves and your enjoyings?
             Do we not beg to be receiv'd your servants?
             To kiss your hands (or if you will vouchafe)
             Your lips, or your embraces?

HILLIARD   We now beg,
             That we may fetch the rings and priest to
                                             marry us
             Wherein are we no beggars?

RACHEL   That will not serve. Your time's not come for
             that yet. You shall beg victuals first.

VINCENT   Oh, I conceive your begging progress is to
             ramble out this summer among your father's
             tenants; and 'tis in request among
             gentlemen's daughters to devour their
             cheesecakes, apple pies -

HILLIARD   Cream and custards -

VINCENT   Flapjacks and pan-puddings.

MERIEL   Not so -

HILLIARD   Why so we may be a kind of civil beggars.

RACHEL   I mean stark, errant, downright beggars, ay,
             Without equivocation; statute beggars.

MERIEL   Couchant and passant, guardant, rampant
             beggars.

VINCENT   Current and vagrant -

HILLIARD   Stockant, whippant beggars!

VINCENT   Must you and we be such? Would you so have
               it?

RACHEL   Such as we saw so merry, and you concluded
               Were th'only happy people in a nation.

MERIEL   The only free men of a commonwealth;
               Free above scot-free; that observe no law,
               Obey no governor, use no religion,
               But what they draw from their own ancient
                                                    custom,
               Or constitute themselves, yet are no rebels.

RACHEL   Such as of all men's meat and all men's
                                                    money
               Take a free part; and, wheresoe'er they travel,
               Have all things gratis to their hands provided.

VINCENT   Coarse fare most times.

RACHEL   Their stomach makes it good;
               And feasts on that which others scorn for
                                                    food.

MERIEL   The antidote, content, is only theirs.
               And, unto that, such full delights are known,
               That they conceive the kingdom is their own.

VINCENT   'Fore Heaven I think they are in earnest, for
               they were always mad.

HILLIARD   And we are madder than they, if we should
               lose 'em.

VINCENT   'Tis but a mad trick of youth (as they say) for
               the spring or a short progress: and mirth may
               be made out of it, knew we how to carry it.

RACHEL   Pray, gentlemen, be sudden.

HILLIARD   We are most resolutely for you in your
               course.

VINCENT   But the vexation is how to set it on foot.

RACHEL   We have projected it; search you the means -
                we have puzzl'd 'em.

MERIEL   I am glad on't. Let 'em pump.

VINCENT   Troth, a small stock will serve to set up
                withal. This doublet sold off o' my back
                might serve to furnish a camp royal of us.

HILLIARD   But how to enter or arrange ourselves into the
                crew will be the difficulty. If we light raw
                and tame amongst 'em (like cage birds among
                a flight of wild ones) we shall never pick up a
                living, but have our brains peck'd out.

VINCENT   We want instruction dearly.

                (*Enter* SPRINGLOVE.)

HILLIARD   Oh, here comes Springlove. His great
                benefactorship among the beggars might
                prefer us with authority into a ragged
                regiment presently. Shall I put it to him?

RACHEL   Take heed what you do. His greatness with
                my father will betray us.

VINCENT   I will cut his throat then. My noble
                Springlove, the great commander of the
                beggars, the very king of canters, we saw the
                gratitude of your subjects in the large
                tributary content they gave you in their
                revels.

SPRINGLOVE   Did you sir?

HILLIARD   We have seen all with great delight and
                admiration.

SPRINGLOVE   I have seen you too, kind gentlemen and
                ladies and overheard you in your quaint
                design to new create yourselves out of the
                worldly blessings Heaven has bestow'd upon

you, to be partakers in those vile courses,
which you call delights, taken by those
despicable and abhorred creatures.

VINCENT   Thou art a despiser, nay a blasphemer
Against the maker of those happy creatures.
Who made 'em such, dost think? Or why so
happy?

RACHEL   (*aside to* MERIEL) He grows more zealous in
the cause than we: sure he'll beg indeed.

HILLIARD   Art thou an hypocrite, then, all this while?
Only pretending charity, or using it
To get a name and praise unto thyself.

MERIEL   (*aside to* RACHEL) They will outbeg the very
beggars.

SPRINGLOVE   But are you, ladies, at defiance too,
With reputation and the dignity
Due to your father's house and you?

RACHEL   Hold thy peace, good Springlove, and though
you seem to dislike this course, do not betray
us in it; your throat's in question. I tell you
for goodwill, good Springlove.

MERIEL   What wouldst thou have us do? Thou talk'st
o'th' house. 'Tis a base melancholy house.
Our father's sadness now banishes us out on't.
And for the delight thou tak'st in beggars and
their brawls, thou canst not but think they live
a better life abroad than we do in this house.

SPRINGLOVE   I have sounded your faith and am glad I find
you all right. And for your father's sadness,
I'll tell you the cause on't - which I learn'd
from his merry mate Master Hearty. He was
this morning told by some wizard that you
both were born to be beggars -

RACHEL   How?

SPRINGLOVE   For which he is so tormented in his mind, that
               he cannot look upon you but with heart's
               grief.

VINCENT   This is most strange.

RACHEL   Let him be griev'd then till we are beggars.
               We have just reason to become so now;
               And what we thought on but in jest before,
               We'll do in earnest now.

SPRINGLOVE   Oh, I applaud this resolution in you; would
               have persuaded it; will be your servant in't.
               For, look ye, ladies: The sentence of your
               fortune does not say that you shall beg for
               need, hunger or cold necessity. If therefore
               you expose yourselves on pleasure into it, you
               shall absolve your destiny nevertheless, and
               cure your father's grief. I am overjoy'd to
               think on't; and will assist you faithfully.

RACHEL   A Springlove! A Springlove!

SPRINGLOVE   I shall prepare you now for the adventure,
               Give rules and directions. I will be your
                                               guide.
               Your guard, your convoy, your authority.
               You do not know my power, my command
               I'th' beggar's commonwealth.

VINCENT   But how came this to be, good Springlove?

SPRINGLOVE   I'll confess all.
               In my minority, your father bred me
               At school and took me to his service after
               He had pluck'd me from the road, a naked
               Beggar. You may
               Remember how through seven summers I
               Would go to visit distant kinsmen, but these
                                               were
               Pretexts. I spent those times indulging
               Of my secret pleasure which was begging,
               Led to't by nature. My indulgent master,

When cold and hunger forc'd me back at
                                  winter,
Reciev'd me still again till, two years since,
He being drawn by journey toward the north
Where I was quarter'd with a ragged crew,
On the highway, not dreaming of him there,
I did accost him with a "Good your Worship,
Please give of one small penny to a cripple
And God will give it back to you in Heaven."

(*All laugh.*)

Yet he, with searching eyes through all my rags
And counterfeit postures, made discovery
Of his man, Springlove; chid me into tears
And a confession of my forespent life.
At last, upon condition *that* vagary
Should be the last, he gave me leave to run
That summer out. In autumn back came I
To my home clothes and former duty.
Such was your father's wish to keep me here,
That he conferred his steward's place on me,
Which clogg'd me this last year from those
                                  delights
I would not lose again to be his lord.

GIRLS   A Springlove! A Springlove!

SPRINGLOVE   Pursue the course you are on then. Till you
Have been beggars, the sword hangs o'er your
                                  father.
And I'll provide a progress of such pleasure
That our sovereign's court could never boast
In all its tramplings on the country's cost;
Whose envy we shall draw, when they shall
                                  read
We outbeg them, and for as litle need.

ALL   A Springlove! A Springlove!

SPRINGLOVE   Follow me, gallants, then, as cheerfully.

ALL   We follow thee.

(*Exeunt.*)

Scene Four

Justice

Justice Clack's *house*. Clack *supervises* Sentwell *and* Nugent.

CLACK   Come, sirs, hasten to make the court ready, for I have but one prisoner to try and would gladly have her arraigned, condemned and punished before our wedding guests - may the good Lord shrink their bellies - arrive. Bring the prisoner in at a double pace, Master Sentwell.

         (Sentwell *goes*.)

         Observe, Master Nugent, that I am ever mindful of those gentlemen who reproach the law for its slowness and have made it my business to place expedition before justice.

         (Sentwell *leads in the prisoner*, Joan Cope. Nugent *makes ready to write down the proceedings*.)

         And a-hey, we are in session. Master Sentwell, speak clearly and in a firm tone of the manner of the apprehension of the prisoner.

SENTWELL   Justice Clack, your worship. The prisoner, Joan Cope, was apprehended in the act of begging in the village of Apperknowle, and, when taken, there was discovered on her person -

CLACK   Speak out, tell us how much was discover'd.

SENTWELL   Three ha'pence, your worship, gleaned, so we believe, from her mendicant activity.

CLACK   "Mendicant activity" is good, Master
                 Sentwell. Have you writ down "mendicant
                 activity" Master Nugent?

NUGENT   I have, your worship.

CLACK   A-hey, then all is well. Continue, Master
                 Sentwell.

SENTWELL   Notwithstanding that the parish of the
                 prisoner lies in the town of Walsall in
                 Warwickshire where relief is provided for her,
                 she did make a journey into the county of
                 Nottinghamshire, knowing she would become
                 a charge upon the parishes of that county.

CLACK   Say "a charge and a burden" rather, Master
                 Sentwell.

SENTWELL   Your worship. A charge and a burden upon
                 the parishes of that county.

CLACK   Have you writ down "a charge and a burden",
                 Master Nugent?

NUGENT   I have your worship.

CLACK   A-hey-hey, then pray continue, Master
                 Sentwell.

SENTWELL   I have concluded, your worship.

CLACK   Then you have made an end of speaking in
                 this matter.

SENTWELL   I have, your worship.

CLACK   Have you writ down that Master Sentwell has
                 made an end of speaking, Master Nugent?

NUGENT   I have, your worship.

CLACK   A-hey-hey-hey, then 'tis my turn at last. Thou
                 runagate, beggar and vagrant. Thou hast heard
                 what has been witnessed against thee by the

honest gentleman. That thou wast
apprehended and so forth, that when taken,
there was discovered from mendicant activity
and so forth. That notwithstanding and so
forth, a charge and a burden. Littera scripta
manet. Does anything remain to be said?

JOAN   Your worship, may I speak a few words in my
        defence?

CLACK   So long as they are few. For Master Nugent
        will have to write them down, and he is not a
        clerk by profession, but merely in loco clerico
        for my clerk Martin who is today vanish'd
        into what thin air we know not; and 'tis
        tedious work for a man not accustom'd in it to
        preserve in ink and paper the effluvia of the
        undeserving poor. Have you writ that down,
        Master Nugent?

NUGENT I have, your worship.

CLACK   Then, prisoner, speak to the point, with a
        brevis esse laboras and a-hey.

JOAN   Your worship, I have three small children that
        cannot fend for themselves, of which one is
        lame, and have nothing to live upon but the
        charity of good people. I -

CLACK   Hast thou three children? Thou art but a
        young woman to have three children.

JOAN   Your worship, I am eighteen.

CLACK   Hast thou writ down three children, the one of
        them lame, Master Nugent?

NUGENT I have, your worship.

CLACK   And where is your husband?

JOAN   Your worship, he is gone before me into
        Newcastle to find work -

CLACK	What is his calling?
JOAN	We have been tenant farmers, your worship, but being dispossessed of our holding, I was -
CLACK	No, no, no. I asked not what was his calling in the past but what is it now, for tempora mutantur, nos et mutamur in illis and a trololly lolly.
JOAN	This is what I was saying your worship -
CLACK	Come on, then out and say it. If the prisoner will not answer questions, we shall ne'er be through our business. Has he any visible means of support?
JOAN	Your worship, he has journeyed north and has found work, mining the coal in Newcastle.
CLACK	Works he under the ground then ?
JOAN	Your worship, he does.
CLACK	Then his means of support is not visible. A-hey! Have you writ that down, Master Nugent?
NUGENT	I have, your worship.
JOAN	He sent word that I was to come to him with our children. But the money he sent down never come, like someone thieved off with it, your worship. But I had to come anyhow, money or no.
CLACK	This is such a story as any vagabond can tell, as easy invented as forgotten. Thou shalt be stripped naked to the waist and whipped back to thy parish, where thou shalt remain, taking only that portion of relief that is thine and not burdening other citizens with thy needs of bread and drink. Take her away!

JOAN
But I must go north to my husband, not back to my parish. I was only begging for bread for my children for that night, and we was to be on our way up north and out of your part the next day -

CLACK
Take her away!

(SENTWELL *removes* JOAN.)

And you may write down, Master Nugent, that I would not ha' been so lenient had it not been my niece's wedding day. Have you writ that down?

NUGENT
Not yet, your worship, for you are still a-saying of it.

CLACK
And yet when I think of the quantities of sack and roasted meats I must today stand account for, and those mostly to be guzzled by strangers, I am sore tempted to haul the huswife back and administer savage justice on her.

NUGENT
'Tis as you please, sir.

CLACK
I know 'tis as I please. This is my house, this is my court. Why, if 'tis not what a man pleases, then a-hey, hey nonny and so forth!

(OLIVER *comes in followed by* SENTWELL.)

OLIVER
Father, father -

CLACK
Oliver, my son, I perceive from your manner and countenance that you are the bearer of ill tidings.

OLIVER
I am indeed, sir -

CLACK
But what can it be, something pertaining to Amie, my niece -

OLIVER   Sir, Amie is -

CLACK   Some mishap with my niece which prevents
              the match -

OLIVER   Sir, your clerk, Martin -

CLACK   And I do suspect Martin, my clerk is a party
              to this -

OLIVER   Sir, they have run away -

CLACK   I suspect the pair of them have run away
              together, and this on her wedding morning.
              Why did you not tell me this?

OLIVER   Father, I have been trying to tell you this -

CLACK   Master Nugent, thou hast not, I hope, writ this
              down.

NUGENT   I have not, your worship.

OLIVER   Father, I have dispatch'd -

CLACK   Peace, Oliver, how shall we proceed if we
              both talk at once? Where are they gone?

OLIVER   We know not, father, but I have dispatch'd
              riders -

CLACK   Send out riders in all directions, ask who saw
              them along the way -

OLIVER   Sir, I have -

CLACK   This brings disgrace upon our family and puts
              me at the mercy of the Tallboys who are
              mighty i' the shire. With my clerk? We must
              o'ertake them before they find a parson or I
              will be grandsire to a pack of inky-fingered
              bratlings.

OLIVER	They stole away, it seems, at dawn and could by now -
CLACK	Be far afield, quite. Then pursue 'em and pursue 'em again. We cannot have the country plunging into chaos.
OLIVER	I will attend to it father.
CLACK	You shall do more than attend! If you do but attend, then I'll be no more judge; and forty pound a year men will smirk behind their cloaks as I ride past. The devil take attend; no, sir you shall hasten, harry, hustle and hey-hey. Bring 'em back or your year's allowance stands in forfeit.
OLIVER	My allowance? What brings that into question?
CLACK	My whim. Go fetch the runagates, or you ride not horse nor bear gold coin this year.
OLIVER	Sir -
CLACK	My humour is the law, away!

(OLIVER *goes*.)

CLACK	Sentwell, do you and Nugent on the instant travel North -
SENTWELL	We will, sir.
CLACK	I myself will send order to the kitchens to pluck the meats from the turnspit and send the sack back to the cellar. No bride, no wedding; no wedding no hospitality. In the wake of elopement thrift. Write that down, Master Nugent, then away-hey-hey !!

(CLACK *sweeps off, followed by* NUGENT, *still scribbling and* SENTWELL.)

SCENE FIVE

Merriment

Enter RANDALL *holding a purse.*

RANDALL   Well, go thy ways, Springlove. If ever any
              just or charitable steward was commended,
              sure he shall be at the last quarter day. Here,
              in this bag, is five and twenty pounds for this
              quarter's beggar charge. And (if he return not
              by the end of this quarter) here's order to a
              friend to supply for the next. Five and twenty
              pounds! This is the heaviest bag I ever toted
              in my life, and in my youth I was bearer of
              my Lady Retford's bonnet-boxes. If I now
              should turn this money to mine own use! Ha!
              Dear devil tempt me not. To rob the poor is a
              poor trick; every churchwarden can do't. But
              something whispers me that my master for his
              steward's love will supply the poor however I
              may handle the matter. Then I rob the steward
              if I restore him not the money at his return.
              Away temptation, leave me. I am frail flesh;
              yet I will fight with thee. But say the steward
              never return. Oh, but he will return. Perhaps
              he may not return. Turn from me, Satan;
              strive not to clog my conscience. I would not
              have this weight upon't for all thy kingdom.

              (*Enter* OLDRENTS *and* HEARTY, *drinking.*)

HEARTY   (*singing*) 'Hey down, hey down and down.'
              No. that was not the manner of it. 'Hey down,
              hey down' and . . . 'Remember, sir, your
              covenant to be merry'.

OLDRENTS   I strive to be so. Yet something pricks me
              within. You see yon sour-faced fellow.
              Something troubles him. Can he force mirth
              out of himself, how think you? Why, how now
              Randall? At your duties, still, where's
              Springlove?

RANDALL Of the man, sir, I know not. But here is his money. I pray that I be charged with it no longer. The devil and I have strain'd courtesy these two hours about it. I would not be corrupted with the trust of more than is my own. Mr. Steward gave it me, sir, to order it for the beggars. He has made me steward of the barn and them while he is gone (he says) a journey to survey and measure lands. Some purchase, I think, for your worship.

OLDRENTS I know his measuring of land. He is gone his old way. And let him go. Am not I merry, Hearty?

HEARTY Yes, but not hearty merry. There's a whim now.

OLDRENTS The poor's charge shall be mine. Keep you the money for him.

RANDALL No, sir, I beg you sir. I have not had it so many minutes as I have been in several minds about it, and most of them dishonest.

OLDRENTS Go then, and give it to one of my daughters to keep for Springlove.

RANDALL Oh, I thank your worship.

(RANDALL *goes*.)

OLDRENTS   Alas, poor knave!
How hard a task it is to alter custom!

HEARTY And how easy for money to corrupt it.
What a pure treasurer would he make!

OLDRENTS All were not born for weighty offices.
Which makes me think of Springlove.
He might have ta'en his leave though.

HEARTY Springlove?
I hope he's not run off with some large trust.
I never lik'd such demure, downlook'd
fellows.

OLDRENTS You are deceiv'd in him.

HEARTY Not I. You cannot
Change dog-daisies into roses: you pluck'd
Him from a common ditch and set him at
The centre of your garden; well he's wither'd.

OLDRENTS Hearty, enough, I say you are deceiv'd.

HEARTY Take but the instance of t'other day.
I, by some chance, was passing by your
kitchen,
Just as the meats were standing to be carv'd.
And there I heard your Springlove give the
order
For a quail to be unjointed!

OLDRENTS Where's th'offence?
Did the quail hang too long 'twixt the pantry
and
The spit?

HEARTY No, no, the bird was succulent.
The fault lies in the word: unjoint a quail?
Pox o' that. Unjoint a bittern: a quail
Should be display'd.

OLDRENTS How exact you are.

HEARTY Well 'tis your steward's function to possess
At his fingers' ends his proper verbs for
carving.
Thus: your swan is lifted but your goose
Is rear'd: How can
A fellow savour quail when 'tis unjointed,
Not display'd.

OLDRENTS 'Tis the same quail all the while:
Two wings, two legs, a giblet disposition.

HEARTY   •   When gentles eat their roasted quail
unjointed:
They sup as beggars 'mongst the unanointed.

OLDRENTS   Hearty, my brain turns swiftly melancholic
Under the burden of your niceties.

HEARTY   Then, friend Oldrents, will I now recite
If't please you.

OLDRENTS   Orator, speak on.

HEARTY   There was an old fellow at Waltham Cross
Who merrily sung though his joy was all lost.
He never was heard to sigh with "Hey-ho,"
But sent it out well with a "Haigh trolly lo."
He cheer'd up his heart when his goods went
to ruin
With a "Heghm, boys, heghm and a cup of old -"
But where's the rhyme there? "Went to ruin",
"Cup of old . . ." No, no. "Went to the devil,
cup of. . ."

(*Enter* RANDALL. *He still carries the bag.*)

RANDALL   Good Master Oldrents, sir. My mistresses are
both abroad.

OLDRENTS   How? Since when?

RANDALL   On foot sir, two hours since, with the two
gentlemen their lovers. Here's a letter they
left with the butler. And, sir, there's a
mutt'ring in the house.

OLDRENTS   I will not read, nor open it; but conceive
Within myself the worst that can befall them;
That they are lost and no more mine. What
follows?
That I am happy; all my cares are flown,
So I may now incline to jovial mirth,
Which I will force out of my spleen so freely,
That grief shall lose her name where I have
being;

And sadness, from my furthest foot of land
Where I have life, be banish'd.

HEARTY   What's the whim now?

OLDRENTS

My tenants shall sit free this twelvemonth;
And all my servants have their wages
                 doubled;
And so shall be my charge in housekeeping.
I hope my friends will find and put me to't.

HEARTY

For them I'll be your undertaker, sir.
But this is overdone. I do not like it.

(OLDRENTS *turns to* RANDALL.)

OLDRENTS

And for thy news, the money that thou hast
Is now thine own. I'll make it good to
                 Springlove.
Be sad with it and leave me. For I tell thee,
I'll purge my house of stupid melancholy.

RANDALL

I'll be as merry as the charge that's under me.

(*A confused noise within of laughing and
singing, and one crying out.*)

The beggars, sir. Do'ee hear 'em in the barn?

OLDRENTS

I'll double their allowance too, that they may
Double their numbers and increase the noise:
These bear not sound enough; though one
                 (methought)
Cried out among 'em.

RANDALL

By a most natural cause. For there's a doxy
Has been in labour, sir. And 'tis their custom
With songs and shouts to drown the woman's
                 cries,
A ceremony which they use, not for
Devotion, but to keep off notice of
The work they have in hand. Now she is in
The straw, it seems; and they are quiet.

OLDRENTS   We will have such a lying in, and such
                  A chris'ning, such upsitting and gossiping!
                  I mean to send forty miles' circuit at the least
                  To draw in all the beggars can be found,
                  And such devices we will have for jollity
                  As fame shall boast to all posterity.
                  Am I not merry, Hearty? Hearty merry?

HEARTY   Would you were else. I fear this overdoing.

OLDRENTS   We will have such a festival month on't,
                  Randall -

RANDALL   Sir, you may spare the labour and the cost;
                  They'll never thank you for't. They'll not
                                                    endure
                  A ceremony that is not their own,
                  Belonging either to the child or mother.
                  A month, sir? They'll not be detained so long
                  For your estate. Their work is done already:
                  The bratling's born; the doxy's in the
                                                    strummel,
                  Laid by an autem mort of their own crew,
                  That serv'd for midwife; and the childbed
                                                    woman
                  Eating of hasty pudding for her supper,
                  And the child, part of it for pap,
                  I warrant you, by this time; then to sleep,
                  So to rise early to regain the strength
                  By travel, which she lost by travail.

OLDRENTS   Can this be?

RANDALL   She'll have the bastard at her back tomorrow
                  That was today in her belly, and march a
                                                    footback
                  With it. And for the crew you'll find 'em
                  At their high feast already.

HEARTY   Pray, let's see 'em, sir.

SCENE SIX

Ecstasy

RANDALL *opens the scene. The* BEGGARS *are discovered. A tableau around* CICELY *who has just given birth. Music: 'Frummagem Rummagem'.*

CICELY	Pretty child with fifteen fathers, Each as wild as any other; Pretty child pray would you rather Wapping mort was not your mother?
	Will you live through fifteen summers, While the winter snow may clean you: Will old Nick and fifteen drummers Take you from me 'ere I wean you?
ALL BEGGARS	(*singing*) Frummagem rummagem cackle and crow, Beggar is born and beggar is bred; Frummagem rummagem let him grow Then hang him all except his head.
YOUNG BEGGAR	I'm youth.
ALL	'Tis fair.
YOUNG BEGGAR	I'll fly.
ALL	To where?
YOUNG BEGGAR	The highest steeple I can find I'll steal.
ALL	Take care.
YOUNG BEGGAR	Your eyes.
ALL	You dare.
YOUNG BEGGAR	While clever hands will rob you blind.

ALL	Frummagem rummagem whistle and hiss,
	He'll climb the heavens for his peck;
	Frummagem rummagem take his piss,
	And hang him by his pigeon's neck.
SLY BEGGAR	I'm glib.
ALL	'Tis true.
SLY BEGGAR	And sly.
ALL	That too.
SLY BEGGAR	The fullams dance upon my spin
	Take heed.
ALL	We do.
SLY BEGGAR	Your gold.
ALL	Eschew.
SLY BEGGAR	When cross you lose and pile I win.
ALL	Frummagem rummagem shiver and shit
	He'll catch a parrot with his tongue;
	Frummagem rummagem take his wit
	And watch him gargle when he's hung.
SOLDIER	I'm stout.
ALL	'Tis so.
SOLDIER	And strong.
ALL	We know.
SOLDIER	I'm master of the bloody stuff
	My work.
ALL	Clubs ho!
SOLDIER	Is found.
ALL	A blow.

SOLDIER   When clever words are not enough.

ALL   Frummagem rummagem gabble and croak,
               He'll face an army with his fist;
               Frummagem rummagem take his oak,
               Then hang him up and let him twist.

               Frummagema rummagema frummagema
                                        rummagema,
               Frummagema rummagema rum rum rum.

OLDRENTS   Good heaven, how merry they are.

HEARTY   Be not you sad at that.

OLDRENTS   Sad, Hearty, no, unless it be with envy
               At their full happiness. What is an estate
               Of wealth and power, balanc'd with their
                                                freedom,
               But a mere load of outward compliment.

HEARTY   I ha' not so much wealth to weigh me down.

OLDRENTS   True, my friend Hearty, thou having less than I
               Art the merrier man;
               But they exceed thee in that way so far
               That should I know my children now were
                                                beggars
               (Which yet I will not read), I must conclude
               They were not lost, nor I to be aggriev'd.

               (*One of the beggars looks out and sees*
               OLDRENTS *and* HEARTY.)

1ST BEGGAR   Tour out with your glaziers!

2ND BEGGAR   I swear by the ruffin
               That we are assaulted by a queer cuffin.

               (*Some panic among the beggars. Some make
               ready to go, others improvise weapons, some
               hold their ground.*)

RANDALL   Hold! What d'you mean, my friends?

PATRICO	This is our master. The master of your feast and feasting house.
BEGGAR	Is this the gentry cove?

(*The beggars react. Those what were flying return. A majority crowd towards* OLDRENTS *in gratitude. Some return to their food. One or two show sullen defiance.*)

BEN	Lord bless his worship.
MEG	His good worship.
LIZ	Bless his worship.
PATRICO	Now bounteous sir, before you go Hear me, the beggar Patrico; Or priest, if you do rather choose That we no word of canting use.
HEARTY	Your fortune-teller again. Would he could prophecy himself away from here.
OLDRENTS	Peace, Hearty.
PATRICO	Long may you live, and may your store Never decay nor balk the poor And as you more in years do grow, May treasures to your coffers flow; And may your care no more thereon Be set, than ours are that have none. But as your riches do increase, So may your heart's content and peace.
HEARTY	'Tis a good vote sir Patrico, but you are too grave. Let us hear and see something of your merry grigs, that can sing, play gambols and do feats.
PATRICO	Sir, I can lay my function by And talk as wild and wantonly As Tom or Tib or Jack and Jill

When they at bowsing ken do swill.
Oh I can make you see and hear;
But oft my dreams occasion fear.

HEARTY   I have no fear of you, sir.

PATRICO   Well, well, very well. (*To the* BEGGAR CREW.)
We must do feats, sirs, a merry grig, a
gambol.

(*The* BEGGARS *lay aside the remains of the
feast and make ready for the dance. The* CREW
*begin to dance. The ringleaders are those who
shunned* OLDRENTS *when he was introduced.
The most subservient skulk at the back,
unwilling to join in at first, but subsequently
drawn in by the frenzy of the others. The
dance begins as a formal circle but gradually
becomes a frightening display of uninhibited
energy. It is not directed at* OLDRENTS *and*
HEARTY. *Rather, it gains in power by wilfully
ignoring them. At times, the dancers launch
themselves into the air as if trying to smash
down the beams of the barn with their heads.
Each dancer is in an individual trance, not
aware of any other individual, but drawing on
a communal pool of energy and ecstasy. The*
SHORT-HAIRED BEGGAR *comes forward and,
holding a bible in the air, shouts a frenzied
text. Others join in, speaking when the spirit
moves them. The dance ends suddenly with no
formal climax, and the participants skulk back
to their places, indifferent.*)

HEARTY   How find you, sir, yourself?

OLDRENTS   Wondrous merry, my good Hearty. Do they
not dance in the strangest manner you ever
saw?

HEARTY   Sure, 'tis not your minuet, or 'Jenny Come
Tie My Cravat', and so forth.

OLDRENTS	Indeed. And he that hath the cropped head, did he not speak in a curious manner.
HEARTY	Most curious indeed.
PATRICO	Faith, sirs, I fear our beggars have displeas'd with this their overbold display.
OLDRENTS	No, sir, they have quite enraptured me.
PATRICO	I think we have in all our store Something that could please you more. The old or autem mort's asleep But before the young ones creep Into the straw, sir, if you are (As gallants sometimes love coarse fare, So, it be fresh and wholesome ware) Dispos'd to doxy, or a dell That never yet with man did mell; Of whom no upright man is taster, I'll present her to you, master.

(JOAN COPE, *now with the crew, is beckoned forward*.)

OLDRENTS	Away! You should be punish'd. Oh!
HEARTY	How is it with you, sir?
OLDRENTS	A sudden qualm overchills my stomach, but 'twill away.

(*The* PATRICO *addresses the* CREW.)

PATRICO	You have done well. Now let each tripper Make a retreat into the skipper, And coach a hogshead, till the darkman's pass'd; Then all with bag and baggage bing awast.
OLDRENTS	Take that amongst you.

(OLDRENTS *gives the* PATRICO *money which he distributes. The* BEGGARS *exit*.)

HEARTY What is't he said?

RANDALL That they will be gone tomorrow, sir. Just as I prophesied.

(OLDRENTS *is in a trance.*)

HEARTY How do you think, sir? Or what? Do you fall aback? Do you not know the danger of relapses?

OLDRENTS Good Hearty, thou mistak'st me. I was thinking upon this Patrico. And that he has more soul than a born beggar in him.

HEARTY Rogue enough though, to offer his what-d'ee call-its? His doxies. Heart and a cup of sack, do we look like old beggar-nigglers? Do we seem of the loose kind of gentleman that might throw good coinage at the feet of some broad-buttocked moll for her to bounce and toss us i' the straw? Some young morsel - not altogether clean - who . . .

OLDRENTS Pray forbear your language, good Hearty, you do forget yourself.

HEARTY Will you then talk of sack that can drown this sighing? Sack. Will you in to supper, sir, and take me there your guest? Or must I creep into the barn among your welcome ones?

OLDRENTS You have rebuk'd me timely and most friendly. Come away.

(OLDRENTS *goes.* HEARTY *turns to* RANDALL.)

HEARTY Would all were well with him.

(HEARTY *follows* OLDRENTS *off.*)

RANDALL With him? I would rather all were well with me. I have been carrying this sack of gold back and forth the better part of a day like a stale pudding at a Whitsun fair. The Devil bids me filch it. I fight him off. He bids me again, I quoth "Get thee behind me." A third time he tempts me and I smite him down. Then comes my master: "Take it, take it, 'tis thine." I am perplex'd. Is this the just reward of honesty or yet another curse? For now I know not what to do on't. If I should stow it 'neath my bed, I'll then be in a perpetual sweat that it will be stolen by some varlet o' the house and be hurtling to my mattress every hour like one with th' sleeping sickness. Oh a curse upon poverty and a curse upon wealth too. I could in an instant now turn Anabaptist and proclaim the end of property from the top of a barrel. I cannot bear these shifting times; I am all for order and degree. But what if there is no order? When gentlefolk do sport the rags of beggars and beggars count their piles of gold like the miser i' the adage, where then is order and degree? And banditry and whoring stalk the land, together with the making of comic faces behind the backs o' the clergy. I once could go from one December's end to another without a sniff of temptation. Now a man might break all ten commandments before breakfast and no-one turn a hair. Well, the world is madder and faster than I knew it. I'll retire to my chamber and brood an hour upon the curse of sudden wealth.

(RANDALL *goes.*)

SCENE SEVEN

Amateurs

Enter VINCENT *and* HILLIARD *in rags.*

HILLIARD Is this the life that we admir'd in others, with envy at their happiness?

VINCENT	I would thy mistress heard thee.
HILLIARD	I'm glad she cannot, for I know there is no altering our course before they make the first motion.
VINCENT	Is't possible we should be weary already? And before their softer constitutions of flesh and blood?
HILLIARD	They are the stronger in will, it seems.

(*Enter* SPRINGLOVE.)

SPRINGLOVE	How now, comrades! Repining already at your fulness of liberty? Do you complain of ease?
VINCENT	Ease, call'st thou it? Did'st thou sleep last night?
SPRINGLOVE	Not so well these eighteen months, I swear since my last walks.
HILLIARD	Did not the thunder wake thee?
SPRINGLOVE	Jove, was there thunder?
VINCENT	Nor the noise of the crew in the quarter by us?
HILLIARD	Nor the hogs in the hovel that cried till they drown'd the noise of the wind? I never dream'd a beggar's life so stuffed with affliction.
VINCENT	We look'd upon them in their jollity and cast no further.
HILLIARD	Yet 'twas not jollity alone that drew us forth (by your favour, Vince), but our obedience to our loves, which we must suffer till they cry home again. Springlove, are they not weary yet?

SPRINGLOVE	They have more moral understanding than so. They know this is your birthright into a new world, and everyone knows that we all come crying into the world, even though the whole world of pleasures is before us. The world itself would never have been glorious had it not first been a confused chaos.
HILLIARD	Are they ready to appear out of their privy lodgings in the pig's palace of pleasure?
VINCENT	I left 'em almost ready, sitting on their pads of straw, helping to dress each other's heads (the one's eye is the t'other's looking glass) with the prettiest coil they keep to fit their fancies in the most graceful way of wearing their new dressings that you would admire.
VINCENT	I hope we are as gracefully set out. Are we not?
SPRINGLOVE	Indifferent well. See where they come.

(*Enter* RACHEL *and* MERIEL *in rags.*)

RACHEL	Have a care, good Meriel, to laugh our last gasp out before we discover any dislike or weariness to them. Let us bear it out till they complain first, and beg to carry us home a-pick-pack.
MERIEL	I am sorely surbated with hoofing already though, and so crupper-cramp'd with our hard lodging, and so bumfiddled with the straw, that -
RACHEL	Think not on't. I am numb'd i'the bum and shoulders too, and have found the difference between a hard floor and a down bed with a quilt. But no word, nor a sour look, I prithee.
HILLIARD	Oh here they come now, Madam Fewclothes and my Lady Bonnyrag.

(Rachel *and* Meriel *laugh at the boys in their rags.*)

GIRLS   Ha, ha, ha.

VINCENT   We are glad the object pleases ye.

HILLIARD   Forgive our greedy eyes if looks they steal
On limbs whose rags show more than they
                         conceal.

GIRLS   Ha, ha, ha.

MERIEL   We are glad you are so merry.

VINCENT   Merry and lusty, too. This night will we lie
together as well as the proudest couple in the
barn.

HILLIARD   And so will we. I can hold out no longer.

RACHEL   Does the straw stir up your flesh to't,
gentlemen?

MERIEL   Or does your provender prick you?

SPRINGLOVE   What! Do we come for this? Laugh and lie
                         down
When your bellies are full. Remember, ladies,
You have not begg'd yet, to quit your destiny,
But have liv'd hitherto on my endeavours.
Who got your suppers, pray, last night, but I,
Of dainty trencher-fees from a gentleman's
                         house,
Such as the serving-men themselves
                         sometimes
Would have been glad of? And this morning,
                         now,
What comfortable chippings and sweet
                         buttermilk
Had you to breakfast?

RACHEL   Oh, 'twas excellent!
I feel it good still, here.

MERIEL   There was a brown crust amongst it that has
                made my neck so white, methinks. Is it not,
                Rachel?

SPRINGLOVE   But will you fall to practice? Let me show
                you how to beg. Suppose some persons of
                worth and wealth are passing by here. How
                goes then your maund? 'Tis but for you to
                remember your letter 'R' thrice - respect,
                responsibility and religion. Note me.

                (SPRINGLOVE *accosts two imaginary
                gentlemen.*)

                "Good your good worship" - respect -"your
                charity to the poor" - responsibility - "that
                will duly and truly pray for you day and night "
                - religion.

VINCENT   Oh, very good.

RACHEL   Such a deal of matter in so little space.

MERIEL   And yet, methought, 'twas modest.

SPRINGLOVE   To't again. "Good your good worship, your
                charity to the poor, that will -

ALL   Duly and truly pray for you day and night."

SPRINGLOVE   Only crouch not so low, sirrahs, or your gent
                will not observe the light of piety in your eyes.

MERIEL   I begin to catch the trick on't.

HILLIARD   Prithee, Springlove, hold thy peace and leave
                us to our own genius. If we must beg, let it go
                as it comes, by inspiration. I love not your set
                form of begging.

SPRINGLOVE   Peace. Even on the instant, here come
                passengers. Forget not your rules, quickly
                disperse yourselves and fall to your calling.
                Vincent, stay you here with me.

(*Exeunt* HILLIARD, RACHEL *and* MERIEL. *Enter* SENTWELL *and* NUGENT.)

SENTWELL   (*off, to servant*) Lead the horses down the hill. (*To* NUGENT.) The heat of our speed is over for we have lost our journey.

NUGENT   Had they ridden this way, we had overtaken 'em, or heard of 'em at least.

SENTWELL   But some of our scouts will light on 'em, the whole country being overspread with 'em.

NUGENT   There never was such an escape else.

VINCENT   A search for us perhaps. Yet I know not them, nor they me, I am sure.

SENTWELL   That a young gentlewoman of her breeding, and heir to such an estate, should fly from so great a match and run away with her uncle's clerk!

NUGENT   Old Justice Clack will run mad upon't, I fear.

VINCENT   If I were about to be hang'd now, I could not beg for my life.

SPRINGLOVE   Step forward and beg handsomely, I'll set my goad in your breech else.

VINCENT   What shall I say?

SPRINGLOVE   Have I not told you? Now begin.

VINCENT   After you, good Springlove.

SPRINGLOVE   Good, your good worships.

SENTWELL   Away, you idle vagabond -

SPRINGLOVE   Your worship's charity to a poor critter well starv'd.

VINCENT	That will duly and truly pray for ye.
NUGENT	You counterfeit villains, hence.
SPRINGLOVE	Good masters' sweet worship, for the tender mercy of -
VINCENT	Duly and truly pray for you.
SENTWELL	You would be well whipp'd and set to work, if you were duly and truly serv'd.
SPRINGLOVE	Good worshipful masters' worship, to bestow your charity, and to maintain your health and limbs -
VINCENT	Duly and truly pray for you -
SPRINGLOVE	Vincent, hold your peace, 'tis like begging with a parrot on my shoulder.
VINCENT	I know no other words.
NUGENT	Begone, I say, you impudent, lusty young rascals.
SENTWELL	I'll set you going else.
	(*He hits* SPRINGLOVE *with his switch.*)
SPRINGLOVE	Ah, the goodness of compassion to soften your hearts to the poor.
VINCENT	May we not hit them back?
SPRINGLOVE	'Tis better policy to submit. Ah the sweetness of that mercy, to move your compassion to the hungry when it shall seem good unto you - ah, ah -
NUGENT	Come back, sirrah. His patience and humility have wrought upon me.
VINCENT	Duly and truly pray for you -

NUGENT	Not you, sirrah. The t'other - You look like a sturdy rogue.

SPRINGLOVE	Lord bless you, Master's worship.

NUGENT	There's a halfpenny for you. Let him have no share with you.

VINCENT	(*aside*) I shall never thrive o' this trade.

SENTWELL	They are of a fraternity and will share, I warrant you.

SPRINGLOVE	Never saw him before, bless you, good master, in all my life. (*To* VINCENT.) Beg for yourself. Your credit's gone else. (*To* SENTWELL *and* NUGENT.) Good hea'en to bliss and prosper ye.

(SPRINGLOVE *goes.* VINCENT *pursues the gentlemen.*)

NUGENT	Why dost thou follow us? Is it your office to be privy to our talk?

VINCENT	Sir, I beseech you hear me. - ('Slife, what shall I say?) - I am a stranger in these parts, and destitute of means and apparel.

SENTWELL	So methinks. And what o' that?

VINCENT	Will you therefore, be pleas'd, as you are worthy gentlemen, and blest with plenty -

NUGENT	This is courtly!

VINCENT	Out of your abundant store, towards my relief in extreme necessity to furnish me with a small parcel of money, five or six pieces, or ten, if you can presently spare it.

(SENTWELL *and* NUGENT *draw their swords.*)

NUGENT	Stand off!

SENTWELL	Here's a new way of begging!
VINCENT	Quite run out of my instruction.
NUGENT	Some highway thief that forgets he is weaponless.
VINCENT	Only to make you merry, gentlemen, at my unskilfulness in my new trade. I have been another man i' my days. So I kiss your hands.

(VINCENT *runs off.*)

SENTWELL	What a rakeshame was that. He kisses our hands with his heels.
NUGENT	There is some mystery in his rags. But let him go.

(*Enter* OLIVER, *putting up his sword.*)

SENTWELL	What, Master Oliver, are you drawn as well?
OLIVER	I am, good Sentwell, but not in pursuance of our runagates. I have this moment been begged of by a counterfeit lame rogue, but in such language, the high sheriff's son of the shire could not have spoke better. He asked me if I could spare him ten or twenty pound. I switch'd him; his cudgel was up. I drew, and into the wood he 'scap'd me.
NUGENT	We had such another begg'd of us. The court goes a-begging, I think.
OLIVER	Troubled times indeed when the mendicants plead in rhyming heptameters.
SENTWELL	Met you no news of your kinswoman Amie?
OLIVER	No sign nor report. And you?
SENTWELL	The scent is cold, Master Oliver, but they are only two on foot and we are some two score a' horseback.

OLIVER   Such young wenches will have their own ways
                in their own loves, what matches soever their
                guardians make for 'em. And I hope my father
                will not follow the law so close to hang his
                clerk for stealing his ward with her own
                consent. It may breed such a grudge - in these
                days of strife - that some clerks will be mov'd
                to hang their masters.

NUGENT   But what says Tallboy to the matter, the
                bridegroom that should ha' been?

OLIVER   Marry, he says little to the purpose, but cries
                outright. I like him for that: he holds his
                humour, a miserable wretch though rich.

SENTWELL   I ha' known him cry when he has lost but
                three shillings at mumchance.

OLIVER   Now gentlemen, do you keep on the high road
                here, past the farm. I will search this
                woodland here and - if I enjoy no fortune - I
                must take our sobbing Master Tallboy on to
                Squire Oldrents'. Clerk Martin had some
                private haunts near there unless I am mistook.
                Search on and diligently.

SENTWELL   We do your pleasure.

                (SENTWELL *and* NUGENT *exit.*)

OLIVER   My pleasure and all the search that I intend
                is, by hovering here, to take a review of a
                brace of the handsomest beggar-bitches that
                ever grac'd a ditch or hedgeside. I passed by
                'em in haste, but that one glance possessed
                me with such urges that I must - What the
                devil must I? A pair of beggars? Well, why
                not? Beggars are flesh and blood and rags are
                no diseases. Their lice are no French fleas,
                and there is much wholesomer flesh under
                country dirt than city painting, and less
                danger. I durst not take a touch at London,
                both for the present cost and fear of an after-

reckoning. But Oliver, dost thou speak like a
gentleman? Fear price or pox, ha? Marry, I do
sir. So beggar-sport is excusable in a young
country gentleman, all the more so, since the
charge of bastard-making cannot be laid at his
door by a woman of no means. Rather do the
poor whores sometimes steal the children of
other folks, that they may move compassion
in the breasts of all beholders. He feeds a
beggar-wench well that fills her belly with
young bones. And these reasons considered,
good master Oliver - s'lid here they come.

(*Enter* RACHEL *and* MERIEL.)

They are delicately skin'd and limb'd. There,
there, I saw above the ham as the wind blew.
Now they spy me.

RACHEL   Sir, I beseech you look upon us with the
                favour of a gentleman. We are in a present
                distress, and utterly unacquainted in these
                parts, and therefore forc'd by the calamity of
                our misfortune to implore the courtesy -

MERIEL   - or rather charity -

RACHEL   - of those to whom we are strangers.

OLIVER   Very fine, this!

MERIEL   Be therefore pleas'd, right noble sir, not only
                valuing us by our outward habits -

RACHEL   - which cannot but appear loathsome or
                despicable unto you -

MERIEL   - but as we are forlorn Christians, and, in that
                estimation, be compassionately moved to cast
                a handful or two of your silver, or a few of
                your golden pieces unto us, to furnish us with
                linen and some decent habilements -

OLIVER   Sure, the beggars today are bewitch'd into a
              language they understand not. The spirits of
              some decay'd gentry talk in 'em sure.

RACHEL   May we expect a gracious answer from you, sir?

MERIEL   Our virgin prayers for you would be as
              propitious as you could wish.

RACHEL   That you never be denied a suit by any
              mistress.

MERIEL   Nay, that the fairest may be ambitious to
              place their favours on you.

RACHEL   That your virtue and valour may lead you to
              the most honourable actions, and that the love
              of all exquisite ladies may arm you.

MERIEL   And that when you please to take a wife, may
              honour, beauty and wealth contend to endow
              her most.

OLIVER   Pray, tell me how long have you been
              beggars, or how chanc'd you to be so?

RACHEL   By influence of our stars, sir.

MERIEL   We were born to no better fortune.

OLIVER   How came you to talk thus, and so much
              above the beggars' dialect?

RACHEL   Our speech came naturally to us -

MERIEL   - and we ever lov'd to learn by rote as well as
              we could.

RACHEL   And to be ambitious above the vulgar -

MERIEL   - to ask more than common alms -

RACHEL   - whate'er men please to give us.

OLIVER   (*aside*) What a tempting lip that little rogue moves there! And what an enticing eye the t'other. I know not which to begin with. What's this, a flea upon thy bosom?

MERIEL   Is it not a straw-coloured one, sir?

OLIVER   Oh what a provoking skin is there? That very touch inflames me.

RACHEL   Sir, are you mov'd in charity towards us yet?

OLIVER   Mov'd? I am mov'd. No flesh and blood more mov'd.

MERIEL   Then pray, sir, your benevolence.

OLIVER   (*aside*) Benevolence? Which shall I be benevolent to, or which first? I am puzzl'd in the choice. Would some sworn brother of mine were here to draw a cut with me.

RACHEL   Sir, noble, sir.

OLIVER   First, let me tell you, damsels, I am bound by a strong vow to kiss all of woman sex I meet this morning.

MERIEL   Beggars and all sir?

OLIVER   All, all. Let not your coyness cross a gentleman's vow, I beseech you.

(*He kisses* RACHEL.)

RACHEL   You will tell now.

OLIVER   Tell, quoth-a! I could tell a thousand on those lips - and as many upon these!

(*He kisses* MERIEL.)

Milk from the cow steams not so sweetly. I must lay one of 'em aboard; both if my tackling hold.

GIRLS   Sir. Sir.

OLIVER   But how to bargain, now, will be the doubt.
             They that beg so high as by the handfuls may
             expect for price above the rate of good men's
             wives.

RACHEL   Now, will you, sir, be pleas'd?

OLIVER   With all my heart, sweetheart. And I am glad
             thou knowest my mind. Here is twelvepence
             apiece for you.

GIRLS   We thank you, sir.

OLIVER   That's but in earnest. I'll jest away the rest
             with ye. Look here, you can have all this.

             (OLIVER *shows them money.*)

             All this. Come, you know my meaning. Dost
             thou look about thee, sweet little one? I like
             thy care. There's nobody coming. But we'll
             get behind those bushes. I know you'll keep
             each other's counsels. Must you be drawn
             to't? Then I shall have to pull. Come away -

GIRLS   Ah, ah -

             (*Enter* SPRINGLOVE, VINCENT *and* HILLIARD.)

VINCENT   Let's beat his brains out.

OLIVER   Come leave your squealing.

RACHEL   Oh, you hurt my wrist.

HILLIARD   Or cut the lecher's throat.

SPRINGLOVE   Would you be hang'd? Stand back, let me
             alone.

MERIEL   You shall not use us so.

SPRINGLOVE   Master! Do not hurt 'em!

OLIVER   Hurt 'em? I mean only to do good. Shall I be
            prevented?

SPRINGLOVE They be but young and simple. And if they
            have offended, let not your worship's own
            hands drag 'em to the law. Correct 'em not
            yourself, it is the beadle's office.

OLIVER   Do you talk, shake-rag? 'Sblood, yond's more
            of 'em. Pox o' their rheumy eyes, I shall be
            beggar-maul'd if I stay. - Thou say'st right,
            honest fellow; there's a tester for thee.

            (OLIVER *exits, running.*)

VINCENT   He is prevented and asham'd of his purpose.

SPRINGLOVE Nor were we to take notice of his purpose
            more than to prevent it.

HILLIARD   True, politic Springlove. 'Twas better his own
            fear quit us of him, than our force.

RACHEL   What? Will you not follow the rogue and beat
            his brains out?

SPRINGLOVE 'Twere not advis'd. He has his kinsmen and
            we are but poor beggars with no refuge in the
            law.

            (*Pause.* SPRINGLOVE *exits to watch* OLIVER'S
            retreat.)

RACHEL   Look you here, gentlemen, twelvepence
            apiece, besides fair offers and large promises.
            What ha' you got today, gentlemen?

VINCENT   More than (as we are gentlemen) we would
            have taken.

HILLIARD   Yet we put up with it in your service.

            (*Re-enter* SPRINGLOVE.)

MERIEL	Ha, ha, ha, switches and kicks.
SPRINGLOVE	Talk not here of your gettings. We must quit this quarter. That venereal gentleman's repulse may arm and return him with revenge on us. We must, therefore, leap hedge and ditch now, till we 'scape out of this liberty to our next rendezvous, where we shall meet with the Patrico and his crew, and then, hay toss and laugh all night.
MERIEL	As we did last night.
RACHEL	Hold out, Meriel.
MERIEL	(*to* SPRINGLOVE) Lead on, brave general.
VINCENT	They are in heart still. Shall we go on?
HILLIARD	There's no flinching back, you see.
SPRINGLOVE	And if you beg no better you shall not 'scape the jail or the whip for long.
VINCENT	To tell you true, I have sent up prayers for our arrest. 'Tis like to be the only way to be released from our trade.
	(*Enter* MARTIN *and* AMIE *in poor habits.*)
SPRINGLOVE	Stay, here come more passengers. Single yourselves again, and fall to your calling discreetly.
HILLIARD	I'll single no more. If you'll beg in full cry, I am for you.
MERIEL	Ay, that will be fine; let's charm all together.
SPRINGLOVE	Stay first and list a little.
MARTIN	Be of good cheer, sweetheart; we have scap'd hitherto, and I believe that all the search is now retir'd and we may pass safely forwards.

AMIE	I should be safe with you. But that's a most lying proverb that says "Where love is, there's no lack." I am faint and cannot travel further without meat.
MARTIN	We'll venture at the next vilage to call for some. The best is, we want no money.
AMIE	I fear we shall be taken there. I'd rather starve to death.
MARTIN	Be not so fearful.
AMIE	Would I could beg, rather than buy of those that would betray us.
MARTIN	Yonder be some that can teach us.
SPRINGLOVE	This is the young couple of runaway lovers that your gentleman were so vexed for. Observe my maund and follow.

(SPRINGLOVE *approaches* MARTIN *and* AMIE.)

	Now the Lord come with ye, good loving master and mistress; your blessed charity to the poor, lame and sick, weak and comfortless, that will night and day -
ALL	Duly and truly pray for you. Duly and truly pray for you.
SPRINGLOVE	Hold your peace! I beg like one in an echoing valley. - Good young master and mistress, a little comfort amongst us all, and to bless you where e'er you go, and -
ALL	Duly and truly pray for you. Duly and truly -
SPRINGLOVE	Hold your peace and let me alone! - Now sweet young master and mistress, to look upon your poor, that have no relief or succour, no bread to put in our heads -

(All begin to beg together.)

VINCENT	No lands or livings.
MERIEL	No bands or shirts, but lowsie on our backs -
HILLIARD	No smocks or petticoats to hide our scratches.
RACHEL	No shoes to our legs, or hose to our feet.
ALL	Duly and truly pray for you.
SPRINGLOVE	I'll run away from you if you beg a stroke more. Good worshipful master and mistress -
MARTIN	Good friend forbear. Here is no master or mistress. We are poor folks. Thou seest no worship upon our backs, I am sure. And for within, we want as much as you, and would as willingly beg, if we knew how as well.
SPRINGLOVE	Alack for pity. I have some food here, and what I have is yours if you'll accept it. 'Tis wholesome food from a good gentleman's gate - Alas good mistress. Much good do your heart. *(Aside.)* How savourly she feeds!
MARTIN	What do you mean, to poison yourself?
AMIE	Do you show love in grudging me?
MARTIN	Nay, if you think it hurts you not, fall to. I'll not beguile you.
AMIE	This beggar is an angel, sure!
MARTIN	And here, mine host, something towards your reckoning.
SPRINGLOVE	Nothing by way of bargain, gentle master. 'Tis against order and will never thrive. But sir, I'll take your reward in charity.
MARTIN	Here then, in charity. This fellow would never make a clerk.

SPRINGLOVE	What? All this, master?
AMIE	What is it? Let me see't.
SPRINGLOVE	'Tis a whole silver threepence, mistress.
AMIE	For shame, ingrateful miser. Here, friend, a golden crown for thee.
SPRINGLOVE	Bountiful goodness! Gold? If I thought a dear year were coming, I would take a farm now.
AMIE	I have robb'd thy partners of their shares, too. There's a crown more for them.
ALL	Duly and truly pray for you.
MARTIN	What have you done? Less would have serv'd. And your bounty will betray us.
AMIE	Fie on your wretched policy.
SPRINGLOVE	No, no, good master. I knew you all this while, and my sweet mistress too. And now I'll tell you. The search is every way; the country all laid for you. 'Tis well you stay'd here. Your habits, were they but a little nearer our fashion, would secure you with us. But are you married, master and mistress? Are you joined in matrimony? In heart I know you are. And I will (if it please you) bring you to a curate, that lacks no licence, nor has any living to lose, that shall put you together.
MARTIN	Thou seem'st to me a heavenly beggar!
SPRINGLOVE	But yet this curate is so scrupulous and severely precise, that unless you, mistress, will affirm that you are with child by the gentleman, or that you have, at least, cleft or slept together, he will not marry you. But if you have, then 'tis a case of necessity and he holds himself bound to do it.

MARTIN   You may say you have.

AMIE   I would not have it so, nor make that lie
              against myself for all the world.

SPRINGLOVE   (*aside*) That I like well, and her exceedingly.
              - I'll do my best for you, however. The seven
              of us are now become a crew; and our
              safety's greater (since we are all pursu'd) in
              greater number still. Accordingly we will hop
              hedge and ditch to Mapledown where tonight
              I'm pledg'd to meet the good Patrico's crew;
              and in their ragged bosom shall we hide.
              Come, bing awast!

VINCENT   Bing awast? What language speak you here?

RACHEL   He has turned Dutchman in an instant.

SPRINGLOVE   No, 'tis not Dutch, it is the beggar's tongue,
              Or (as they call it) canting. "Bing awast!"
              Is but your call to go, as one would say:
              "Come sirrahs, quit this quarter, let's away."
              If all you gentle folk would beggars turn,
              You must forget your world, another learn:
              'Tis not home merely you have left behind:
              But language, morals, certainty of mind.

              (*Music: 'Bing Awast'*. RACHEL *and* MERIEL *try
              to make* AMIE *more like a beggar;* VINCENT
              and HILLIARD *do the same for* MARTIN.
              SPRINGLOVE *acts as an intermediary between
              the* BOYS *and* GIRLS.)

GIRLS   For we who are born to the satin and silk
              Now are gaily foresworn of sweet oysters and
                                                    milk;
              So we venture abroad thence to scavenge and
                                                    bilk
              'Midst the cuffins and bawds of itinerant ilk.

BOYS   The velvets and lace of the gentlest of men
              Should scarce find their place in the rude
                                                bousing ken:

Nor could travel the land glad of strummel
                                        for bed
Till pretension's abandoned and finery fled.

ALL Endowed with no gift for this verbiage rare
Come-uppance is swift should we tread in dull
                                        care;
With some phrases of canting must arm for
                                        the fray
Bing awast! Come a-ranting! Let's up and
                                        away!

GIRLS Of manners and morals a change is afoot,
Must cast out such quarrels as prudish may put.

BOYS When rogues proffer jockam in bousiest prank,
Must not let it shock 'em, but take by the
                                        shank and give it a wank.

GIRLS Take by the shank and give it a what?

BOYS Take by the shank and give it a wank.

GIRLS The cardinal's hat! Well pray fancy that.

BOYS The rumpscuttle's duties lay akin to the stew
Must relinquish our beauties to the fine
                                        derring-do?

GIRLS No words of concision could formerly speak
Of the sweetest incisions of lads at their peak
                                        with pizzles of teak.

BOYS Lads at their peak with pizzles of teak?

GIRLS Lads at their peak with pizzles of teak.

BOYS Cry higgledy piggle, they're vowing to
                                        niggle!

ALL In this jovial crew we're to hell and be
                                        damned
With our certainties few and too hastily
                                        crammed

With a phrase of the canting, we're armed for
                                    the fray:

Bing awast! Come a-ranting! Let's up and away!
Bing awast! Come a-ranting! Let's up and away!
Bing awast! Come a-ranting! Let's up and away!
Bing awast! Come a-ranting! Let's up and away!
Bing awast! Come a-ranting! Let's up and away!
Bing awast! Come a-ranting! Let's up and away!
Bing awast! Come a-ranting! Let's up and away!
Bing awast! Come a-ranting! Let's up and away!
Bing awast! Come a-ranting! Let's up and away!
Bing awast!

Blackout.

Interval.

ACT TWO

SCENE EIGHT

Wooing

AMIE *runs on, breathless, followed by* MARTIN. *She flings herself to the floor, laughing.*

AMIE	I have never known such running! My ankles are more scratches than skin, my feet are thorns and blisters and my garments torn into such beggar-state that I need no disguise!
MARTIN	Sweetheart, I fear the company we have fallen in with -
AMIE	My heart is knocking at my ribs like a hungry visitor at the door!
MARTIN	This fellow Springlove -
AMIE	Oh an excellent fellow, is't not? And a sure and safe guide through hedgeholes and bramble tracks -
MARTIN	I find his company overfamiliar. I have seen a hundred fellows of his kidney hauled before your uncle's presence in the court-
AMIE	But we are now (thanks to his good offices) safe from our pursuers -
MARTIN	Only by falling in the greater trap of this same Springlove. I doubt much mischief in his countenance and manner -
AMIE	Good Martin, hold your tongue and do not hasten so to play the ingrate. Now, I am taken with a raging thirst from all this up and down scambling. There is a farmhouse over yonder, and, if you lov'd me, you would hasten there and beg a jug of water -

MARTIN   It will not be safe -

AMIE   You err too much o' the side of caution. Go
                      and do my bidding, or I will never under
                      God's sun abide the ceremony you would
                      have me undergo.

MARTIN   Mistress, you ha' made your choice and now
                      must follow down the road we took together
                      yesterday at dawn.

AMIE   Of that, I'll be the judge. Go to't and fetch
                      me water quick, before you are betrothed to a
                      wrinkled corpse.

                      (MARTIN goes, AMIE sits up.)

AMIE   I have not had such a frolic since I was a girl
                      and played at touch and scurry with the
                      village children What a day is this: first to
                      wake in a ditch with the open sky my canopy;
                      then to run hungry into such good company;
                      and last to play the cunning fox o'er hedge
                      and ditch with half the huntsmen in the
                      county at my back. And yet I am in woeful
                      straits. This Springlove's a proper man - and
                      yet perhaps he only seems so. I have made
                      myself desperate running from a despis'd
                      match to one I like but little better and now I
                      am perplex'd. But peace, here he comes. Lie
                      down heart and find a temperate rhythm for
                      your dance.

                      (SPRINGLOVE comes on.)

SPRINGLOVE   Resting when there's begging to be done?
                      This sloth is not the way to stave off hunger.
                      I have dispatch'd our modest, untrain'd crew
                      To gather provender from farmers' wives:
                      And you lie here a'frowsting i' the sun?

AMIE   Oh do not put me to't gentle Springlove.
                      I lack the custom of the open air
                      And find myself (to put it plain) more weary
                      I' the leg than ever since my girlhood.

SPRINGLOVE	Well, since you are beggar from necessity
	Not choice, my teacher's harshness I'll relent.
	(*Aside*.) As who would not when pleas fall
	from such lips?
	But did your uncle Clack not let you roam
	Free as a bird o'er the wilds of his estate?
AMIE	If I was ever bird, I had my wings
	Clipped early, aye, and bars to fence me in.
SPRINGLOVE	And yet you slipp'd your cage and flew
	To freedom: did you grow your wings afresh;
	Or Cupid grant a second pair to exalt
	Young love from dark depths into airy skies?
AMIE	If I am free, well, yet I do not know it.
SPRINGLOVE	'Twill all be as I promis'd: my curate found,
	We'll wed you fast and no man shall presume
	To cleave the pair that you have made
	together.
AMIE	My uncle then will use his lawyer's wiles
	To cut me off from all my just inheritance;
	And I will be condemn'd to live a pauper
	That was wont to flaunt and play the lady.
SPRINGLOVE	And were you happy in your gilded state?
	No, faith, you spoke but moments past of bars
	And bleak captivity. Freedom resides
	In the contented spirit; and without it,
	All the jewels and gewgaws of the wealthy
	Life are but as cumbrances which drag,
	Like friends upon the hanged man's feet,
	To make a quicker end of suffering.
AMIE	And think you I will find in hasty marriage
	To my clerk, the freedom which I crave?
SPRINGLOVE	Faith, where there's love, then freedom is
	assured.
AMIE	And dost thou think he bears a love for me?
SPRINGLOVE	His looks say so and every word agrees.

AMIE   And what of me? Thinks't thou that I could
love him?

SPRINGLOVE   Good Mistress Amie, it has not been much
My business in this world to weigh and
            measure
Goods exchanged, or account for loss and
            profit
In the busy trade of hearts. But still have I
(Ever the observer) kept a ready reckoning
In my head; and I perceive in you
And your young clerk a grave imbalance in
The duties levied and the taxes paid.
He doth shower forth his amorous fund of sighs
And glances, but assimilates from you
A niggard recompense.

AMIE   Sir, you protest your ignorance of love
And then, like a cunning attorney itemise
Each detail of the case against me. Yes, 'tis
            true.
Martin (who in the household long has held
Me dear) has been my means of 'scaping
            marriage
With a man I hate. Yesterday I should have
Wed one Master Tallboy, a fellow fitter
For a clothespole than a husband. Martin,
I fear, have I us'd badly and now,
Knowing not which way to turn, I chide
Him as the instrument of all my woes,
When he (in large measure) has been my
            saviour:
But I cannot love him: not through the
            difference in
Our stations (such niceties of rank bear little
Weight with me), but from the discrepancies
Which lie between our souls: there rests nor
            peace
Nor spirit's freedom in unbalanc'd love.

SPRINGLOVE   But what of your uncle? When
He makes his catch, your fate will be

Enforc'd despite of all your wishes and
                                  desires.

AMIE   And so, I fear, 'twill prove: but thenceforward
I'll ne'er be troubled with the puzzlement
Of choice: my fate being in my uncle's hands
My mind no more I'll scourge with thoughts
                              of freedom.

SPRINGLOVE   What talk is this? Fie on't. Once I have lodg'd
Us with the begging crew, you've made your
                              escape
From marriage, uncle, all the chains that hold
You down and make of sweet young life
                              misfortune.

AMIE   And trust my fate to you, a begging rogue
With whom my acquaintance is but two hours
                              old?

SPRINGLOVE   You reprove me justly (though I gib at rogue)
But I am not a man whose nature can
Be grasp'd by inventory of his travelling rags.

AMIE   'Tis true: you talk above your begging rank
Your disposition's kind and all your manner
Speaks a gentler state than you would own.

SPRINGLOVE   Well, you have confess'd your life to me,
And I would be a churl that did not make
Equal return: though lowly born, I am
The steward of Squire Oldrents.
Through impulse of my heart
And spirit, I seek my freedom in the spring
By trav'lling in this manner, taking adventure
Where I will and food where I can beg it.

AMIE   And your gentle vagabond companions?

SPRINGLOVE   Are Oldrents' daughters and their childhood
                              loves.

(AMIE *laughs*.)

AMIE   So in the company of such a crew, I should
                Find safety.

SPRINGLOVE   Thou shoul'dst. My life I'll stake upon't.

AMIE   But still I know you not.
                Is't not strange that you, who are of age
                To be a husband should seek this freedom
                                                    (which
                You laud so much) in the pleasures of your
                                                    boyhood.
                Do not the forests pall, the meadows' colours
                Fade with each succeeding year compared
                With riper pleasures of the hearth and heart?

SPRINGLOVE   My lady, I assure you, no such thing.
                Why this spring has been (in all my years) the
                                                    most

                Look'd out for, the height of all my travelling
                                                    pleasure.

AMIE   Sir, my acquaintance in the world has been
                Constrain'd, but yet I know so much that if
                I had a friend whose will it was to love you,
                I could tell her how she might succeed
                Her suit and win you to her with her cunning.

SPRINGLOVE   It is not possible: I am not the stuff
                Of Cupid's dreams, being rough in manner
                And too singular in my purpose for
                The disposition of the female sex.

AMIE   No life is set forever
                On an unending road: the ways divide,
                The choice is made, and lo, a different path
                Guides on the traveller to an unknown place.

SPRINGLOVE   And this is how you'd teach your friend to
                woo me.

AMIE   No faith, I would tell her of a man, part gentle
                And part beggar whose mind and spirit could be
                Gain'd by giving him the freedom that he runs

From home to find. I would tell her thus:
Change your heart into a verdant field,
Your conversation to the melody
Of birds, your mind into the open road
That wanders where it will and your sweet
body
To the fragrant hedgerow, hung about
With flowers: then, methinks, you'd win him.

SPRINGLOVE   Faith, such a beauty would indeed ensnare
Me heart and soul; have you such a friend?

AMIE   Oh sir, not I, my life has known but poor
Companionship; I know only myself.

SPRINGLOVE   Perhaps in knowing of yourself, you'll find
Such qualities as you frame in your mind
For this imagin'd friend, whose face I miss;
But were she here, I'd greet her with a kiss.

(SPRINGLOVE *moves towards her. They kiss for a second. Suddenly* VINCENT, HILLIARD, RACHEL *and* MERIEL *come on.*)

VINCENT   Sirrahs, both, hasten. We are pursued.

HILLIARD   The gentlemen whom we had thought lost on
another path are fast approaching.

RACHEL   More rogues to hurt and humble us.

MERIEL   Pray tell, good Springlove, which way should
we fly?

(MARTIN *comes back with a pitcher of water.*)

SPRINGLOVE   The hunt is on, but yet, good fellow foxes, are
we not bold quarry?

VINCENT   Bold we may be, but they a' horseback hold
th'advantage.

SPRINGLOVE	Only while they hold fast to the road. The brambles are our bosom friends and we will plunge amongst 'em. Bing awast!
ALL	Bing awast!

(SPRINGLOVE, VINCENT, HILLIARD, MERIEL *and* RACHEL *dash off.* AMIE *makes to follow, but* MARTIN *holds her back.*)

AMIE	Unhand me, Martin. Our foe is fast upon us.
MARTIN	So I would have it. I had rather stand and endure the wrath of the law then hide in brambles with a crew of vagabonds.
AMIE	If they should seize us, all is lost.
MARTIN	All is now lost for me whether they take us or no. You bear no love for me, but us'd me only as your instrument of freedom.
AMIE	My plight was desperate!
MARTIN	And so was mine. But now 'tis ten times worse.
AMIE	Hide now or else the wrath of law falls on your young shoulders!

(AMIE *breaks free and follows the others.* MARTIN *stands.*)

MARTIN	I traded my secure position for this calf-love of a wench too high in manners and degree for one of my low standing. Oh thou sorry clerk, that risk'd so much and now has lost all: clerkship, wench and reputation. Still I could fly, but yet if they catch me not today, t'will be tomorrow. I had rather surrender now where yet there may be some hope of bargaining to save my skin.

(SENTWELL *and* NUGENT *come on, swords drawn.*)

SENTWELL   What, clerk Martin? Hast thou no nib for thy defence?

NUGENT   Nor inky pellets to project into our faces.

(MARTIN *pours the jug of water over his head.*)

MARTIN   Do not mock me, masters: there's my surrender.

SENTWELL   A wetter clerk I never saw.

NUGENT   'Sblood, fortune hath showered on him and him alone.

SENTWELL   And where's your highborn darling?

MARTIN   Faith not so far, and yet you'll never catch her.

NUGENT   Why so, you lusty fellow?

MARTIN   They hold the advantage both in number and in speed of foot.

SENTWELL   Yet we'll catch her and a brace of beggars.

MARTIN   What's one or two compared with two and twenty?

NUGENT   How say you, rabbit sucker?

MARTIN   Tonight they purpose to meet with a vagrant crew of their acquaintance. I know the time and place. If you do but prefer me to old Clack for these confidences, then your catch is made, not just of her you seek, but of the rowdy beggar band as well. Do you but enlist the watch and your success is sure. Think on't.

NUGENT   The clerk is slippery.

SENTWELL   But yet it is, at heart, a coward clerk and
             therefore can be trusted. Where meet they
             with the crew?

MARTIN   At Mapledown.

SENTWELL   Then we tonight will thither. And if your luck
             holds, Martin, good Justice Clack may yet
             forswear his hanging disposition.

             Exeunt.

SCENE NINE

Drinking

Outside OLDRENTS' *house.* OLIVER *and* TALLBOY *come on
carrying riding switches.*

TALLBOY   She's gone. Amie is gone. Ay me, she's gone,
             and has me left of joy bereft to make my
             moan. Oh, me, Amie.

OLIVER   Why master Tallboy, art not asham'd to cry at
             this growth? And for a thing that's better lost
             than found, a wench?

TALLBOY   Cry! Who cries? Do I cry, or look with a
             crying countenance? I scorn it, and scorn to
             think on her but in just anger.

OLIVER   So, this is brave now, if t'would hold.

TALLBOY   Nay, it shall hold. And so let her go, for a
             scurvy what-d'ee call't. But something of
             mine goes with her, I am sure. She has cost
             me in gloves, ribbons, scarfs, rings, and such
             like things, more than I am able to speak of at
             this time. Oh -

OLIVER   Because thou can'st not speak for crying. Fie,
              Master Tallboy, again?

TALLBOY   I scorn it again and let her go again, and hang
              herself, and the rogue that's with her. I have
              enough, and am heir of a well known estate,
              and that she knows. And therefore, that she
              should slight me and run away with a wages-
              fellow, that is but a petty clerk and a serving
              man. There's the vexation of it. Oh, there's
              the grief and the vexation of it. Oh -

OLIVER   You, sir. This shifting 'twixt resolution and
              snivelling have I had with you every inch of
              our long journey, which is now at an end here.
              This is Master Oldrents' house, where perhaps
              we shall find old Hearty, the uncle of that
              rogue Martin, that is run away with your
              sweetheart.

TALLBOY   Ay, 'tis too true. You need not put me in mind
              on't. Oh, oh -

OLIVER   Hold your peace and mind me. Leave your
              bawling, for fear I give you correction. This is
              the house, I say where it is most likely we
              shall hear of your mistress and her companion.
              Here comes a minion, make up your face
              quickly.

              (*Enter* RANDALL.)

              Shame not yourself forever, and me for
              company. Come, be confident.

TALLBOY   As confident as yourself or any man. But my
              poor heart feels what lies here. Here. Ay, here
              it is. Oh -

OLIVER   Good morrow, friend. This is Squire Oldrents'
              house, I take it.

RANDALL   Pray, take it not, sir, before it be to let. It has
              been my master's and his ancestors' these

three hundred years, so it is not yet to be let.
But as a friend, or stranger, in guestwise, you
are welcome to it. As is every other
gentleman, peasant, child, cur and vagrant
within a radius of two hundred miles.

OLIVER   Thou speak'st wittily and honestly. But I
prithee, good friend, let our nags be set up;
they are tied up at the post. You belong to the
stable, do you not?

TALLBOY   Not so much as the stable belongs to me, sir. I
pass through many offices of the house sir, I
am the running bailey of it.

OLIVER   Well, sir, we have rid hard, hoping to find the
squire at home at this early time in the
morning.

RANDALL   You are deceiv'd in that, sir. He has been out
these four hours. He is no snail, sir. You do
not know him since he has been new moulded,
so I will tell you all.

OLIVER   Our horses, good friend.

RANDALL   My master is an ancient gentleman and keeps
a fine house, and is prayed for by all the poor
in the country. But he fell into a great
melancholy, upon what cause I know not; for
he had then more cause to be merry than he
has now. For he had two daughters that knew
well to order a house and give entertainment
to gentlemen. They were his housedoves, but
now they are flown, and no man knows how,
why or whither.

TALLBOY   My dove is flown too.

OLIVER   Pray hold your peace or feign some mirth if
you can.

TALLBOY   Let her go, let her go. I care not if I have her,
I have her or no. Ha, ha, ha. Oh, my heart will
break, oh -

OLIVER   Pray think of our horses, sir.

RANDALL   Yond fellow is of the same humour as my
master: this way and that way like a
weathercock in a gale. When my master had
his daughters he was sad; and now they are
gone he is the merriest man alive. Up at five
o'clock in the morning and out till dinner
time. Out again at afternoon and so till supper
time. Skice out this a-way, and skice out that
a-way (he's no snail, I assure you). And
tantivy all the country over, where hunting,
hawking or any sport is to be made, or good
fellowship to be had; and so merry on
occasions you would think he had invented
sack and company.

OLIVER   Our horses, I prithee.

RANDALL   And we, his servants, live as merrily under
him, and do all thrive. I myself was but a silly
lad when I came first, a poor turnspit boy. Oh
yes, 'twas all done by hand in those days,
none of your whirling jacks and such devices
to cozen poor people of meat. And I have
now, without boast, forty pound in my purse,
and am the most senior of all the servants but
one, Master Springlove the steward (bless him
where'er he is). He has a world of means, and
we, the underlings, get well the better by him,
besides the rewards many gentlemen give us
that fare well and lodge here sometimes.

OLIVER   Oh, we shall not forget you, friend, if you
remember our horses before they take harm.

RANDALL   No hurt, I warrant you; 'tis marvellous good
country this for horses.

OLIVER   Is not your master coming, think you?

RANDALL   He will not be long a-coming. He's no snail,
as I told you.

OLIVER | Did you so tell me? Yes, I believe you did.

RANDALL | But of all the gentlemen that toss up the ball, yea and the sack too, the finest is old Master Hearty, a decay'd gentleman, who lives upon his own mirth and my master's means.

OLIVER | I am glad that Hearty is here. Bear up, Tallboy, we are like hounds upon the scent. Now friend, pray let me ask you an important question.

RANDALL | Nay, marry, I dare not. Your horses may take cold and never be good after it. Pray go you into the house.

(RANDALL *goes*.)

OLIVER | A pretty humour!

(*Enter* USHER.)

USHER | Do you stand in the porch, gentlemen? The house is open to you. Pray enter.

OLIVER | We follow you. Come Tallboy, let us test Squire Oldrents' entertainment.

TALLBOY | Nay but there's no entertainment without Amie. Ay me!

OLIVER | Yes, yes, good fellow, but thou bearst all most bravely.

TALLBOY | I am a very Stoic, Master Oliver.

(OLIVER *and* TALLBOY *follow the* USHER. RANDALL *returns*.)

RANDALL | Did'st thou but mark those two gentlemen? The one forever pounding me with his insolent questions and his tittle-tattle. The t'other like a maypole, ten feet tall and streaming. I have tasks, I have occupations.

'Tis not in my nature to stand o' the same
patch of ground forty minutes at a time
discoursing of my great aunt's doings in the
time o' Good Queen Bess. It irks my kibes
past endurance. Had the gentleman but a
quarter the work of the servingman, then we'd
hear complainings and see many changes. But
such thoughts are not good for me; they
unsettle my constitution and then follows
sleeplessness, bad digestion and doubting o'
the foundations of the nation. I'll in and
administer port to my wounds.

(RANDALL *goes. The* USHER *leads* OLIVER *and*
TALLBOY *on.*)

USHER   And this, sirs, is the buttery. I am the usher,
                 and can usher you to this or any room i' the
                 house.

OLIVER   Thank you, sir usher, this room will suffice.
                 Our business is urgent. When can we expect
                 your master to come?

USHER   He's upon coming, sir; and when he comes, he
                 comes apace. He is no snail, I assure you.

OLIVER   I was told so before, sir. No snail! Sure 'tis
                 the word of the household and as ancient as
                 the family.

USHER   This gentleman looks sadly, methinks.

TALLBOY   Who, I? Not I. Pray pardon my looks for that.
                 But my heart feels what's what. Ay me -

USHER   I have been usher here these twenty years, sir,
                 and have got well by my place for using
                 strangers respectfully. Something comes in by
                 the by, besides standing wages, when visitors
                 are content with our services.

OLIVER   So, he has given the hint.

(OLIVER *tips the* USHER. *The* BUTLER *comes in.*)

USHER   And here comes our butler.

BUTLER   You are welcome, gentlemen. Please ye take a
                  morning drink in a cup of sack?

OLIVER   In what please you, sir. We cannot deny the
                  courtesy of the house in the master's absence.

BUTLER   He'll come apace when he comes. He's no
                  snail, sir.

OLIVER   Still 'tis the houseword.

BUTLER   No gentleman's house in this county or the
                  next so well stor'd and 'tis as fortunate a
                  house for servants as ever was built upon
                  fairy-ground. I, myself, that have serv'd here,
                  man and boy, these four and forty years have
                  gotten together by my wages, my vails at
                  Christmas and my rewards of kind gentlemen
                  that have found courteous entertainment here -

OLIVER   There he is too -

BUTLER   Have, I say, gotten together (though in a
                  dangerous time I speak it) a brace of hundred
                  pounds. And for losses I have had none. I
                  have been a butler these two and thirty years,
                  and never lost the value of a silver spoon -

BUTLER &   - nor ever broke a glass.
USHER

                  (OLIVER *tips the* BUTLER.)

BUTLER   Thank you, sir. White wine and sugar, say you
                  sir? Or had you rather take a drink of brown
                  ale with a toast?

TALLBOY   I know not what to drink. What's best for a
                  broken heart and a frail constitution?

OLIVER   Good, sir, two cups of your sack will serve.

(*The* Butler *goes. The* Cook *comes on.*)

COOK   And welcome, the cook says, gentlemen.

OLIVER   Faith, they come in batallions.

COOK   I'll fetch a cut of the sirloin to strengthen
            your patience till my master comes, who will
            not now be so long, for he's no snail,
            gentlemen.

            (*The* Butler, *the* Usher *and* Randall *come
            bustling on with drinks.*)

OLIVER   Quite, I have often heard so. Here's to you,
            Master Cook.

            (Oliver *tips the* Cook.)

COOK   I am the oldest cook, and of the ancientest
            house, and the best for housekeeping in this
            county or the next. And though the master of
            it write but squire, I know no lord like him.

            (*Enter* Chaplain.)

USHER   My master has arrived, sir, for look, the word
            is come before him.

COOK   The parson has ever the best stomach. I'll dish
            away presently.

            (*The* Cook *goes.*)

RANDALL   Is our master come, Sir Domine?

CHAPLAIN   Est ad manum. Ille non est cochlea.

            (*The* Chaplain *goes.*)

OLIVER   He has the word in Latin. Now, bear up,
            Tallboy.

            (*Enter* Oldrents *and* Hearty.)

OLIVER   This is the squire and Master Hearty whom we
            seek.

TALLBOY   I seek but one, and these fellows resemble her
               not.

OLDRENTS   About with it my lads. Bear up, Hearty!
               What's this, strangers?

OLIVER   Sir, I am come to inform you -

OLDRENTS   Inform me nothing! I care not who you are, so
               long as you are of the eating and drinking
               persuasion. If you are sir, you are welcome.
               Bustle about, boys, bustle the sack about.
               There is a very tall fellow that hath the look
               of Doomsday upon him. Sir, if you can force
               your countenance into a merry fit, y'are
               welcome. Sack, beer, ale and wine we have in
               plenty. And this is as it should be.

OLIVER   It appears you were abroad betimes, sir.

OLDRENTS   I am no snail, sir.

OLIVER   So your men told us. Our business, sir -

OLDRENTS   We know the word not -

OLIVER   I have here a most urgent letter from -

OLDRENTS   Letters do we use for tinder -

               (OLDRENTS *tears up the letter and throws it on
               the floor.*)

TALLBOY   Ah!

OLDRENTS   Oh, mine ears! What was that, a sigh? And in
               my house? Look, has it not split my walls? If
               not, make vent for it. Let it out. I shall be
               stifled else.

OLIVER   He hopes your pardon, sir, his cause
               consider'd.

OLDRENTS   Cause? Can there be cause for sighing?

OLIVER	He has lost his mistress, sir.
OLDRENTS	Ha, ha, ha. Is that a cause? Do you hear me complain the loss of my two daughters?
OLIVER	They are not lost, I hope sir.
OLDRENTS	No more can be his mistress. No woman can be lost. They may be mislaid a litle, but found again, I warrant you.
TALLBOY	Ah!
OLDRENTS	'Ods my life! He sighs again, and means to blow me out of my house. To horse again. Here's no dwelling for me.
HEARTY	I beg you, Oldrents, stay for food and drink.
OLDRENTS	I'll stay, aye, and cure him if I can. Give him more sack to drown his suspirations.

(*The* BUTLER *buttles.* TALLBOY *drinks.*)

OLIVER	Good sir, we have ridden hard to find you and to ask but one question -
OLDRENTS	In this house there is but one question: will you take a cup of sack or no?
OLIVER	I -
OLDRENTS	And do not waste breath giving the answer, for I listen only to yes.

(*The* BUTLER *gives* OLIVER *sack.* OLIVER *takes* HEARTY *to one side.*)

TALLBOY	Sirs, I should have had her, 'tis true. But she is gone, d'e see? And let her go.
OLDRENTS	Well said. He mends now.
TALLBOY	I am glad I am rid of her (d'e see) before I had more to do with her -

OLDRENTS   He mends apace.

OLIVER   (*to* HEARTY) Sir, I do perceive the Squire's
                mind is not dispos'd to melancholy matters,
                but I am chiefly here to inform you that your
                nephew Martin has stol'n my father's ward,
                that gentleman's bride that should have been.

HEARTY   Indeed sir?

OLIVER   Indeed, know you where they may be hiding?

HEARTY   I protest, as I am a gentleman, I know nothing
                of the matter, nor where the pair of 'em may
                be. But as I am the foresaid gentleman, I am
                glad on't with all my heart. Ha! my boy Mat.
                Thou shalt restore our house.

TALLBOY   For should I have married her before she had
                run away (d'ee see), and that she had run
                away (d'ee see) after she had been married to
                me (d'ee see), then I had been a married man
                without a wife (d'ee see). Where now, she
                being run away before I am married (d'ee
                see), I am no more married to her (d'ee see)
                than she to me (d'ee see). And so long as I am
                none of hers (d'ee see) nor she none of mine
                (d'ee see), I ought to care as little for her,
                now she is run away (d'ee see), as if she had
                stay'd with me, d'ee see?

OLDRENTS   Why this is excellent!

TALLBOY   I perceive it now, and the reason of it; and
                how, by consequence (d'ee see) I ought not to
                look any further after her. (*Cries.*) But that
                she should respect a poor base fellow, a clerk
                at the most and a serving man at best, before
                me, that am a rich man at the worst and a
                gentleman at least, makes me -

OLDRENTS   Worse than ever 'twas! Now he cries outright.

HEARTY   That poor base fellow that you speak of is my
                nephew, as good a genleman as yourself.

TALLBOY	I cry you mercy, sir.

| OLDRENTS | You shall cry no mercy, nor anything else here, sir. This is no place to cry in. Nor for any business. You sir, that come on business - |

| OLIVER | It is most pressing, sir - |

| OLDRENTS | My house is for no business but the belly-business. You find not me so uncivil, sir, as to ask you from whence you came, who you are or what's your business. I ask you no question. And can you be so discourteous as to tell me or my friend anything like business. If you come to be merry with me, you are welcome. If you have any business, forget it; you forget where you are else. And so to dinner. |

| OLIVER | Sir, I have been dispatch'd upon this matter by my father, and if I conclude it not successfully, he will cut off my allowance. |

| OLDRENTS | What, there is a fellow in the kingdom has a son and will cut him off? |

| OLIVER | Even so - |

| OLDRENTS | Had I a son, I would so bedeck him in fine clothes and stable him such a string of horses that the world would catch its breath as he rode by in all his glory. What is this monster calls himself a father? |

| OLIVER | Sir, he is a magistrate of the county, one Justice Clack - |

| HEARTY | Justice Clack! I have heard of this Justice Clack, a fellow much talked up for his conceits and whimsies. |

| OLDRENTS | Justice, say you? Do I cut off my daughters - no, but they have cut off me. Where's the Justice in this? And do I speak of this matter? |

No, faith, I have ta'en a vow of silence in't.
And yet this fellow Clack, cuts off his own
son, hurls him out onto the common road with
neither horse nor baggage and dispatches
letters over half the shire bragging his
unnatural behaviour. How like you this,
Hearty?

OLIVER   Sir, he has sent me on an errand to find this
           gentleman's nephew who has absconded with
           the Justice's niece -

OLDRENTS   Loses a niece into the bargain. This fellow
           scatters his kin to the four winds like a
           drunken pamphleteer. Had I yet a family, I
           would cabin them close; so that, on my
           deathbed I would know my blood ran yet and
           I had not sowed all my days on stony ground.

OLIVER   So all our business, sir -

OLDRENTS   Call it not business, I beseech you. We defy
           all business.

TALLBOY   Ay, marry we do, sir. There shall be no
           business from now and henceforward.

OLDRENTS   Grammercy sack. I am much of your mind in
           this cause against your father, and so in
           pursuit of this - we may not call it business -
           in pursuit of this -

TALLBOY   Hopeless, hopeless, hopeless.

OLDRENTS   The word will serve at your insistence, sir, -
           in pursuit of this hopeless, I have made up my
           mind to return with you and upbraid him -

HEARTY   Peace, friend Oldrents, it is a long journey -

OLDRENTS   'Tis but crossing the country two days and a
           night and 'twill buoy up my spirits. Must I,
           alone in all this land, embrace the cause of
           hospitality and good fathership, which have,

since time began, been all the backbone of our
nation. Pax, I ha' made up my mind to pursue
this hopeless and I will not be crossed in it!
You, Hearty, will accompany our journey, and
you too Randall, a good bout of hopeless will
blow the cobwebs from your pasty face.

(*A knocking.*)

Hark! They knock to the dresser. We'll but
dine and away presently. Bear up I say, thou
tall fellow, and you, the much wronged son
and heir.

TALLBOY   I will bear up, I warrant you, d'ee see, sir. But
here's a grudging still.

OLDRENTS   Fear not, sir, soon you shall be hopeless!!

OLIVER   This fellow as a tyrant tops my father:
I'll gladly ride to watch them rail together.

(*Exeunt all except* RANDALL.)

RANDALL   What humour's this now? On a whim to
undertake a journey of some forty miles to see
this lunatic Justice. And then to haul me along
for company? I have not put my carcass to
bed outside the squire's estate this reign, and
now must pass three nights under strange
blankets that I may meet with a mad judge.
Are there not unsound minds enough i' the
household? My master, that was wont to be
the sanest in the kingdom, now endures much
turbulence 'neath his wig; and with light-
headedness come manic whims and despotism.
But what to do? Should the servant still obey
when the master bids him gather shellfish
from the marigold patch? But if he disobeys,
what then? Am I to invent mine own orders?
God above, preserve me from that. I am good
old Randall still, and will run and fetch
though I am ask'd to pluck a peck of apples
from the moon. Nay, I'll go further, I'll cry

my master's virtues up so loud, that no villain
e'er shall cross me. To horse, to horse. I'll be
as unwilling a saddlebag as ever was strapped
to a mare; and yet I'll smile i' the teeth o' the
storm.

(RANDALL *goes. The scene ends.*)

SCENE TEN

Workshop

Noise of music, laughing and singing off. Enter AMIE, RACHEL
and MERIEL.

AMIE   Let us out of the noise as we love our ears.

RACHEL   Yes, and here we may pursue our own
discourse, and hear one another.

MERIEL   Concerning Springlove and yourself, Mistress
Amie.

AMIE   Well, ladies, my confidence in you, that you
are the same that you have protested
yourselves to be, hath so far won upon me
that I confess myself well affected both to the
mind and person of that Springlove. And if he
be (as fairly as you pretend) a gentleman, I
shall easily dispense with fortune.

MERIEL   He is, upon our honours.

AMIE   I have pass'd no affiance to the other
That stole me from my guardian and my match.
Besides, his mind, more clownish than his
                              habit,
Deprav'd by covetousness and cowardice,
Forc'd me into a way of misery
To take relief from beggars.

RACHEL   Springlove is more gentleman by far than he.

Amie	But though he be never so good a gentleman, he shall observe fit time and distance till we are married.
Rachel	Matrimony forbid else (She's taken).

(*Enter* Springlove.)

Springlove	Oh, ladies, the crew sport on, you lose much mirth.
Meriel	We have our own entertainment.

(Springlove *takes* Amie *aside and courts her in a gentle way.* Vincent *and* Hilliard *come on. Throughout the following they imitate the beggars' dancing and maunding.*)

Vincent	I am come about again for the beggars' life now.
Rachel	You are. I am glad on't.
Hilliard	There is no life but it.
Vincent	With them there is no grievance or perplexity; No fear of war, or state disturbances. No alteration in a commonwealth, Or innovation, shakes a thought of theirs.
Rachel	Of ours, you should say.
Hilliard	Of ours, he means. We beggars fear not loss of our estates But lend or give upon command, the whole Strength of our wealth for public benefit.
Meriel	While others, that are held rich in their abundance, (Which is their misery, indeed) will see Rather a general ruin upon all, Than give a scruple to prevent the fall.
Vincent	'Tis only we that live.

RACHEL   I'm glad you are so taken with your calling.
              We are no less. I assure you.

MERIEL   We find the sweetness of it now.

RACHEL   The mirth, the pleasure, the delights. No
              ladies live such lives as we.

MERIEL   Some few upon necessity, perhaps.

VINCENT   (*aside*) They will never be weary.

HILLIARD   Whether we seem to like or dislike, all's one
              to them.

              (SPRINGLOVE *and* AMIE *come to the rest. The*
              BEGGARS *gradually drift on.*)

SPRINGLOVE   I am yours forever. (*To the others.*) Well,
              ladies, you have miss'd rare beggar sport. But
              here come the chief revellers: the soldier, the
              courtier, the lawyer and the actor, who is
              master of the revels.

              (*The* ACTOR *uses his speech to draw the*
              BEGGARS *into a circle around him.*)

ACTOR   From jigging veins of rhyming mother-wits,
              And such conceits as clownage keeps in pay,
              We'll lead you to the stately tent of war,
              Where you shall hear the Scythian
                                        Tamburlaine
              Threatening the world with high astounding
                                                terms,
              And scourging kingdoms with his conquering
                                                sword.
              View but his picture in this tragic glass,
              And then applaud his fortunes as you please.

              (*Some applause, some catcalls.*)

SPRINGLOVE   Thou hast spoken learnedly and acted bravely.

ACTOR	Grammercy, king. This is the prologue to Tamburlaine the Great, and it is my intention that we should rehearse this play (in part for our own sport) but, in addition, that when we stay with gentry, we may please by giving entertainment, and so gain greater profit in the way of food and drink.
SPRINGLOVE	Faith, 'twas a fine speech, good actor, but are there parts for all the crew?
ACTOR	There are, together with a deal of fighting and dumbshow.
SOLDIER	I'll teach all to fight, of dumbshow I know not.
LIZ	But we have our dance for pleasing gentry.
PATRICO	Not so, Liz: our dance caused too much affray at Squire Oldrents'.
LIZ	He gave us money.
PATRICO	It is grown too riotous; this play shall be more seemly.
MEG	Well let us have a play; yet not of wars and battles but ourselves.
COURTIER	There is no such.
ACTOR	Our Tamburlaine would be of ourselves.
LAWYER	I have thought of a play we may do. I want but actors.
HILLIARD	What persons want you? What would you present?
LAWYER	I would present a commonwealth: Utopia, With all her branches and consistencies.
MERIEL	I'll be Utopia; who must be my branches?

LAWYER	The country, the city, the court, and the camp, epitomiz'd and personated by a gentleman, a merchant, a courtier, and a soldier.
SOLDIER	I'll be your soldier. Am not I one? Ha!
COURTIER	And am not I a fashionable courtier?
ACTOR	But who the citizen or merchant?
SPRINGLOVE	I.
VINCENT	And I your country gentleman.
HILLIARD	Or I.
MERIEL	Yet to our moral, we must add two persons, Divinity and Law.
LAWYER	Why, la you now, and am not I a lawyer?
ACTOR	But where's Divinity?
VINCENT	Marry, that I know not. One of us might do that, if either knew how to handle it.
SPRINGLOVE	The Patrico, he'll do it rarely.
PATRICO	I am hedge-priest, after all. And to perform my higher mysteries I will go fetch wine and bread.

(*The* PATRICO *goes off.*)

VINCENT	Sir, lawyer. These parts stand pretty well, but what must our speeches tend to? What must we do with one another?
LAWYER	I would have the country, the city and the court be at great variance for superiority. Then would I have Divinity and Law stretch their wide throats to appease and reconcile

them; then I would have the soldier cudgel
them all together and overtop them all.

SHORT-HAIRED
BEGGAR
Stay. You want yet another person.

HILLIARD
What must he be?

SHORT-HAIRED
BEGGAR
A masterless man. A beggar.

VINCENT
Here's enough of us I think. What must the
beggar do?

SHORT-HAIRED
BEGGAR
He must at last overcome the soldier, and
bring them all to Beggars' Hall.

SOLDIER
Your beggar will never overcome your
soldier.

SHORT-HAIRED
BEGGAR
Oh he will, friend, indeed he must. For when
the parts of your Utopia take up cudgels, the
one against another, and all do turn soldier,
then the sword lays waste and beggary is your
only outcome.

MERIEL
But this is a sad end for our play and for poor
Utopia.

SHORT-HAIRED
BEGGAR
Not so, friend, for there is happiness greater
in beggary than in riches, and when the scythe
cuts, it brings the meek and the mighty to the
same level and the field can then be ploughed
and all begun anew.

ACTOR
Well, you may play the beggar, but yet, since
'tis a Utopia, our ending should methinks be
jolly.

SHORT-HAIRED
BEGGAR
I know no jollier ending than the ploughed
field.

JOAN
If there is to be a lawyer, I would show the
justice who whipped me without reason.

MEG	I would show my hard life, but that's a common tale and no ending to it that anyone knows.
ACTOR	Let us rather our first idea of Tamburlaine. If all pitch in and argue on the substance of the play, then there's no art -
RACHEL	Faith yes, Tamburlaine would inspire us all.
SHORT-HAIRED BEGGAR	Because 'twas your idea -
SPRINGLOVE	The play of Utopia is very well; but we must entertain, not overwhelm our hosts with all the broils of state.
LAWYER	We would but show our lives within a play; where's harm in that?
CICELY	For my child's sake, I would not have a play too sad.
LIZ	Let the bab decide, you'll get more sense -
COURTIER	'Tis merriment we seek to make, not brawl and strife.
MERIEL	Then I should be not Utopia, but St. George; hurrah for England and I will slaughter all our foes.
SHORT-HAIRED BEGGAR	England is Utopia.
JOAN	Not for me.
SHORT-HAIRED BEGGAR	But yet it shall be so; 'tis but to slay the foe within yourself.
ACTOR	All these thoughts can we employ within our Tamburlaine, 'tis but a shifting of the scene -

Liz	From Persia to Mapledown -
Rachel	If you will play St. George, Meriel, then I shall be your wife.
Springlove	I think you never shall agree.
Cicely	Good Springlove, you decide.

(*The* Patrico *comes running on.*)

Patrico	Our quarter is beset. Bing awast, bing awast, the queer cove and the harman-beck.

(*Some of the beggars start to run.*)

Springlove	We are beset indeed. What shall we do?
Vincent	I hope we shall be taken.
Hilliard	If the good hour be come, welcome by the grace of good fortune.

(*Enter* Sentwell *and* Nugent. *Most of the* Crew *slip away.*)

Sentwell	Beset the quarter round. Be sure that none escape.
Springlove	Lord to come with you, blessed master, to a many distressed -
Vincent & Hilliard	Duly and truly pray for you -
Sentwell	A many counterfeit rogues! So frolicsome and so lamentable all in a breath? You were acting a play but now. We'll act with you. Incorrigible vagabonds.
Springlove	Good master, 'tis a holiday with us -
Nugent	Away, rogue, we seek an heiress here -

(SPRINGLOVE *pushes* MEG *forward*.)

SPRINGLOVE An heiress? Why this is an heiress, sir, of some dozen apples a year.

SENTWELL What tell'st me of this, an old beggar woman. We must find a gentlewoman in the bloom of youth.

NUGENT They are outside i' the courtyard, they cannot escape!

(*Exit* SENTWELL, NUGENT *and watch*.)

SPRINGLOVE Bing awast! We'll take our chance through the door.

VINCENT No, good Springlove. The ladies and we are agreed now to draw stakes and play this lousy game no further.

HILLIARD We will be taken, and disclose ourselves. You see we shall be forc'd to it else.

SPRINGLOVE Do you fear no shame, ladies?

RACHEL Dost thou think it a shame to leave begging?

MERIEL Or that our father will turn us out to't again?

SPRINGLOVE Nay, since you are so resolute, know that I, myself, begin to find this no course for gentlefolk.

AMIE Make but your protestations good and take me yours. And for the gentleman that surprises us, though he has all my uncle's trust, he shall do anything for me to our advantage.

HILLIARD I hear their return.

RACHEL We are all of a mind to give ourselves up.

(Re-enter Sentwell *and* Nugent. Nugent
drags on the Courtier Beggar *and hurls him
to the floor.)*

SENTWELL   She's scap'd or is invisible. (*To* Springlove.)
You, sir, I take to be the chief rogue of this
regiment. Let him be whipp'd till he brings
forth the heiress.

NUGENT   That is but till he stinks, sir. Come sir, strip,
strip.

*(*Nugent *tears at* Springlove's *clothing.* Amie
comes forward.)

AMIE   Unhand him, sir. What heiress do you seek,
Master Sentwell?

SENTWELL   Precious, how did my haste o'ersee her?
Mistress Amie, are you safe and well?

AMIE   Better in health and spirit than I ever was
before.

SENTWELL   Could I or your uncle, Justice Clack, ever ha'
thought to find you in such company?

AMIE   Of me, sir and my company, I have a story to
delight you, which on our march towards your
house I will relate to you.

SENTWELL   And thither will I lead you as my guest.
But to the law surrender all the rest:
I'll have them clapp'd in chains and herded
back to justice.

RACHEL   No!

VINCENT   Faith, good sir, among this crew are
gentlefolks, not to be marched in rags and
bonds along the highway in the public gaze -

COURTIER   I am one such sir, a courtier, travelling on the
King's express business.

NUGENT   See how common is their story -

SENTWELL   It is a familiar tale and does naught but
                  disgrace the teller. You, mistress, shall go a
                  horse back -

SPRINGLOVE   I beg you sir, show compassion to these
                  people who are innocent of any crime -

SENTWELL   Thou hast begg'd for long enough and now
                  must attend the settling of thy account with
                  the Law. The rest of you must fare all alike.
                  Lead them away.

MEG   Our life, this is. Our rugged life.

JOAN   You share our sport, now take our lash.

                  (BEGGARS *and* GENTLEFOLK *are led away.*)

NUGENT   Our purpose long enough has been delayed
                  The Law's account falls prompt and shall be
                  paid.

                  Exeunt All.

                  SCENE ELEVEN

                  Road

*Two hours later. Complete darkness. A mournful song in the
distance, 'Donegal'. The stars come out. Some moments.
NUGENT comes on. Behind him, chained together and walking
in procession behind him, are MEG, the PATRICO and CICELY
carrying her baby. They are singing. A little way behind them
come the ACTOR, the COURTIER and LIZ.*

NUGENT   Move onward. You've three miles till you
                  stop.

LIZ   Oi! Harman beck. Your key fit my mortise?

NUGENT   Hold your peace, callet.

(NUGENT *stops. The six* BEGGARS *move onwards and exit through the audience. We hear the song still.* SPRINGLOVE, VINCENT, RACHEL, HILLIARD *and* MERIEL *come on, in chains.* RACHEL *stops and sits, unable to continue.*)

VINCENT   Bear up, Rachel.

RACHEL   I did not reckon with the law's severity when I began the beggar life.

HILLIARD   This was your whim, we but endur'd it for your sakes.

SPRINGLOVE   No, the fault is mine.

NUGENT   Keep moving, or you'll ne'er reach Justice.

MERIEL   And yet, methinks, the stars shone never clearer to my eyes.

(MERIEL *stands looking up at the stars.* RACHEL, SPRINGLOVE, VINCENT, HILLIARD *and* NUGENT *follow the procession off through the audience. The* SHORT-HAIRED BEGGAR, *the* LAWYER, *the* SOLDIER *and* JOAN COPE *come on. They see* MERIEL.)

LAWYER   See how fair Utopia stands alone in chains.

JOAN   Meriel?

MERIEL   I was looking at the stars.

(*They look up.* SENTWELL *comes on.*)

SENTWELL   Keep on the move, there's a long road ahead.

(*The* BEGGARS *still look at the stars. We hear the song in the distance.*)

SHORT-HAIRED   There's freedom, friend.
BEGGAR

(*Some moments. The* BEGGARS *and* SENTWELL
move off. The scene ends.)

SCENE TWELVE

Play

The house of JUSTICE CLACK. CLACK *and* MARTIN.

CLACK   I have forgiven you. Provided that my niece
be safely taken, and so be brought home.
Safely, I say; that is to say, unstain'd,
unblemish'd, undishonor'd; that is to say,
with no more faults, criminal or accusative,
than those she carried with her.

MARTIN   Sir, I believe -

CLACK   Nay, if we both speak together, how shall we
hear one another? You believe her virtue is
armour of proof without your guard, and
therefore you left her in the hands of rogues
and vagabonds to make your own peace with
me -

MARTIN   Mine intent, sir, and my only way -

CLACK   Nay, if we both speak together, how shall we
hear one another, as I said before? What you
would have said had you not been interrupting
me, was that your intent and your only way
was to run away with her; that is to say for
her to shun the match that I had made for her;
that is to say rather to disobey me than to
displease herself. Wherein (although she did
not altogether transgress the law) she did both
offend and prejudice me, an instrument, nay, I
may say, a pillar thereof. And you in assisting
her, did not only infringe the law in an
unlawful departure from your master, but in a
higher point; that is to say, top and top-
gallows high. I would ha' found a jury should
ha' found it so.

MARTIN   But, sir, an't please you.

CLACK   Must we then both speak together? Have I not
              borne with thee, to speak all thou pleasest in
              thy defence? Have I not broke my own rule,
              which is to punish before I examine, and so to
              have the law surer o' my side? And dost thou
              still persist? Hold your own peace; or, as I am
              a justice of the King's, I will unsay what I
              said before and set a Curat Lex at you that
              shall course you up the heavy hill.

              (*Pause.*)

              Oh, is your tongue fallen into your leg now?
              Do not you know I have acquitted you? Go
              your way in, and see that Squire Oldrents and
              his boon companion, who, I think, were got in
              sack, christen'd in sack, nurs'd with sack, and
              fed up to gray hairs with only sack; see, I say,
              that they do not drink all my sack.

              (MARTIN *goes.*)

              My son Oliver (I thank him) has brought me a
              pair of guests. First they heap invective on my
              head for not, in perpetuity, maintaining the
              idle lollop in whores and horses; then they set
              their hearts on turning my cellar into a desert.
              This last hour I have been hard at it, hiding
              the bottles from the servants and the servants
              from the guests.

              (*Enter* SENTWELL *and* NUGENT.)

              Oh, masters Sentwell and Nugent! Good
              news?

SENTWELL   Of beggarly news, the best you have heard.

CLACK   That is to say, you have found my niece
              among the beggars. That is to say -

SENTWELL   True, sir, we have found her -

CLACK   Now, if we both speak together, who shall
             hear one another?

SENTWELL   I thought your desire was to be inform'd.

CLACK   I can inform myself, sir, by your looks. I have
             taken a hundred examinations i' my days, of
             felons and other offenders, out of their very
             countenances; and wrote 'em down verbatim
             to what they would have said. I am sure it has
             serv'd to hang some of 'em and whip the rest.

SENTWELL   (aside) Justice Clack still!

NUGENT   (aside) His clack must only go.

CLACK   But to the point. You have found my niece.
             You have left her at your own house; not only
             to shift her out of her disguise, but out of her
             shame to come no nearer me, until I send her
             pardon.

SENTWELL   Most true, sir, but the company she was in -

CLACK   Again, do I not know the company? Beggars,
             rogues, vagabonds and hedge-birds -

NUGENT   Hedge-players too, your worship.

             (Enter OLIVER.)

OLIVER   Sir, Master Oldrents, in that he enjoys not
             your company begins to doubt of his
             welcome.

CLACK   Was it I that invited him hither? I dispatch'd
             you on pain of your allowance (which now -
             under duress - I have you granted) to retrieve
             an heiress. In her stead you return with two
             guzzling fellows who, in three scant hours,
             have consumed all the liquors scrimp'd from
             the wedding breakfast.

OLIVER   Sir, their own desire brought them hither. I
             but show'd them the way.

CLACK   Then show them the way to sobriety. And tell the Squire I come.

OLIVER   Pray sir, be pleas'd to do so, for he says -

CLACK   Nay, if we both talk together -

OLIVER   Who shall hear one another.

                (OLIVER *goes*.)

CLACK   But are there players among the apprehended?

NUGENT   Yes, sir. And they were contriving a play among themselves, just as we expris'd them.

CLACK   Players! I'll pay them above the rest.

SENTWELL   You shall do well in that, to put 'em in stock to set up again.

CLACK   Yes, I'll put 'em in stocks, and set 'em up to the whipping-post. They can act justices, can they? I'll act a justice among 'em; that is to say, I will do justice upon them with a hey and a trololly!

SENTWELL   But pray sir, as justice, they say, is blind, you may be pleas'd to wink a little. I find that you have merry old gentlemen in your house that are come far to visit you. I'll undertake that these players in a device which they have already studied, and a pack of clothes which I shall supply 'em with, shall give your guests much content.

NUGENT   Aye, sir; and perhaps move compassion in you towards the poor strolls.

CLACK   But you know my way of justice is to punish 'em first and be compassionate afterwards.

SENTWELL   But for your guest's sake, who do favour and affect the quality of actors very much, permit 'em sir.

NUGENT   It will enlarge your entertainment
                exceedingly.

CLACK   And perhaps save me the expense of a runlet
                of sack the while. Well, sir, for that respect
                and upon your undertaking that they shall
                please, I will prorogue my justice on the
                rogues. But, pray, Master Sentwell, as you
                have found my niece, look to her and see her
                decently brought home.

SENTWELL   In her own best apparel. But you must
                prorogue your displeasure to her, too.

CLACK   I will do so until my scarce welcome guests
                be gone.

                (*Enter* RANDALL.)

RANDALL   Sir, my master sends you word, and states
                plainly that without your company your
                entertainment stinks. If you come not at once,
                twice, thrice, he's gone presently, before
                supper. He'll find an host at an inn worth a
                hundred o' you.

CLACK   Good friend, I now will satisfy your master,
                without telling him he has a saucy knave to
                his man.

                (*Exit* CLACK.)

RANDALL   Thank your worship.

SENTWELL   Do you hear, friend? You serve Master
                Oldrents.

RANDALL   I could a' told you that.

NUGENT   Your name is Randall.

RANDALL   Oh forgive me. Are you so wise? I hope
                you're not a witch? How know you that I'm

Randall? Were you ever at my master's house
or at Dunghillford where I was born?

SENTWELL   No, but we have notes to know you by.

RANDALL   I was never twelve mile from thence i' my life
            before this journey. God send me within ken
            of our own kitchen smoke again.

NUGENT   Now, sirrah, tell us the name of your master's
            steward?

RANDALL   Master Springlove an't please you. Know you
            him too?

SENTWELL   And your master's daughters?

RANDALL   Whaw. Mistresses Rachel and Meriel.

SENTWELL   Who are far from home, your master knows
            not where.

RANDALL   Whaw, whaw, whaw. But know you where
            they all are?

SENTWELL   Even here by, at my own house.

RANDALL   Whaw -

NUGENT   Enough, friend. Finding them last night with a
            crew of beggars, we did arrest them and march
            them here in chains to the Justice -

RANDALL   Whaw!

SENTWELL   - not giving credit (there being so many
            counterfeit rogues) to their high-born story -

RANDALL   Whaw, whaw.

SENTWELL   - which you have now confirmed as true.

NUGENT   And we would make amends for our misjudg'd
            cruelty by assisting in their project -

SENTWELL - which is to present themselves cunningly to the squire as actors in the beggars' play.

RANDALL Whaw, whaw, whaw, whaw - why do we not go to 'em then?

NUGENT But secretly. They would surprise your master.

SENTWELL Not a word to anyone.

RANDALL Mum. Will you go then?

(*Enter* MARTIN.)

MARTIN Oh, Master Oldrents' man. Pray let me entreat you into the buttery, it is my master's desire.

RANDALL Oh now, when it is supper-time. To fill my belly with thin drink to save his meat. Shit o' your master. My master's steward's a better man. I'll to him at this gentleman's house and all the rest. Whaw, whaw -

SENTWELL Randall, you forget -

RANDALL But I am mum. I do no not speak of my master's steward, nor of all the rest.

NUGENT Randall!

RANDALL Mum again. Whaw, whaw, whaw, whaw, whaw.

(RANDALL, SENTWELL *and* NUGENT *go*.)

MARTIN The man's as mad as his master. The strangest strangers that ever came to our house.

(*Enter* TALLBOY. MARTIN *and* TALLBOY *look at one another*.)

TALLBOY Well, Martin, for confessing thy fault, and the means thou mad'st whereby she is taken, I am friends with thee. But I shall never look upon her, or thee, but with grief of mind, however I bear it outwardly. Oh -

MARTIN   You bear it very manfully, methinks.

TALLBOY   Ay, you think so, and I know so - But what I feel, I feel. Would one of us two had never both seen the other.

MARTIN   You speak very good sense, sir. And for your comfort, I'll tell you. Mistress Amie is fallen in love with one of the beggars.

TALLBOY   Then have I nothing else to do but laugh as long as I live. Ha, ha, ha - To let a beggar cozen thee of her. Ha, ha, ha. A beggar! I shall die merrily yet. Ha, ha, ha.

MARTIN   Ha, ha, ha!

                (*Enter* CLACK, OLDRENTS, HEARTY *and* OLIVER, *drinking sack.*)

CLACK   A-hey, boys, a-hey. This is right; that is to say, as I would have it; that is to say -

TALLBOY   A beggar. Ha, ha, ha -

MARTIN   Ha, ha, ha -

CLACK   A-hey, boys, a-hey. Master Oldrents, the virtue of your company turns all to mirth and melody, with a-hey trololly lolly lolly. Is't not so, Masters?

OLDRENTS   Why, thus it should be. How was I deceiv'd! Now I see you are a good fellow.

TALLBOY &   Ha, ha, ha.
MARTIN

CLACK   A-hey, boys, a-hey -

HEARTY   What is the motive of your mirth, Nephew
             Martin? Let us laugh with you.

OLDRENTS   Was that spoke like a friend, Hearty? Lack we
             motives to laugh? Are not all things,
             anything, everything to be laugh'd at? And if
             nothing were to be seen, felt, heard or
             understood, we would laugh at it too.

CLACK   You take the loss of your mistress merrily,
             Master Tallboy.

TALLBOY   More merrily than you will take the finding of
             her. Ha, ha, ha. A beggar. Ha, ha, ha.

CLACK   Can I be sad to find her, think you?

MARTIN   He thinks you will be displeas'd with her and
             chide her.

CLACK   You are deceiv'd Master Tallboy; you are
             wide, Master Tallboy, above half your length,
             Master Tallboy. Law and justice shall sleep,
             and mirth and good fellowship ride a circuit
             here tonight. A-hey Master Oldrents, a-hey
             Nephew Tallboy that should ha' been, and
             a-hey for the players. When come they? Son
             Oliver, send for Master Sentwell and his
             company.

OLIVER   (*aside*) This is the first fit that ever he had of
             this disease. Pray God it prove fatal.

TALLBOY   Players. Let us go see too. I never saw any
             players before in my life.

             (*Exit* OLIVER, TALLBOY *and* MARTIN.)

OLDRENTS   But is there a play to be expected and acted
             by beggars?

CLACK   That is to say; yes indeed. They are upon
             their purgation. If they can present anything
             to please you, they may escape the law. If

not, tomorrow, gentlemen, shall be acted
Abuses Stripp'd and Whipp'd among 'em.

(*Enter* Sentwell *and* Nugent.)

A-hey, Masters. Where are your Dramatis
Personae, your Prologus and your Actus
Primus, ha?

SENTWELL   A word an't please you.

(Clack *confers with* Nugent *and* Sentwell
who hands him a piece of paper.)

OLDRENTS   I have not known a man in such a humour.

HEARTY   And of his own finding! He stole it, indeed,
out of his own bottles, rather than be robb'd
of his liquor.

OLDRENTS   He does so outdo us, that we look like staid
men again, Hearty, fine sober things.

HEARTY   But how long will it last? He'll hang himself
tomorrow for the cost we have put him to.

OLDRENTS   I love a miser's feast dearly.

HEARTY   To see how thin and scattering the dishes
stood, as if they fear'd quarrelling.

OLDRENTS   And most suitable to the niggardliness of his
feast, we shall now have a play presented by
beggars.

CLACK   Send 'em in, Master Sentwell.

(Sentwell *goes.* Nugent *ushers the audience
into their places.*)

Sit, gentlemen; the players are ready to enter.
And here's their playbill.

OLDRENTS   'Utopia' or 'The Beggars' Commonwealth'.

HEARTY   With interludes from 'Tamburlaine the Great'.

                (*Enter* TALLBOY, OLIVER *and* MARTIN. *They
                sit.*)

TALLBOY   The players are coming in.

CLACK   A-hey for that.

                (*The* ACTOR *comes on, the rest of the players
                huddle nervously.*)

ACTOR   With jigging veins of rhyming mother-wits,
                And such conceits as clownage keeps in fits,
                We'll lead you to Old England's stately hills
                Where you shall hear how poor St. George is ill,
                Threatened by villains' high astounding words,
                And scourged on all sides by the threatening
                                                        sword.
                View this true story in our comic glass,
                And then applaud his fortunes as we pass.

                (*Some applause.*)

HEARTY   A well-penned prologue.

OLDRENTS   True stories and true jests do seldom thrive on
                stages.

                (*The* CREW, *mostly disguised from head to foot
                in straw Mummers' costumes, enter and take
                up positions around the acting area.* AMIE,
                *dressed in everyday clothes, comes on as the
                Enterer-In. She carries a broom and sweeps
                out an acting area. The mummers chant.*)

AMIE   Open the door and let us in,
                We hope your favour we shall win:
                Room, room, gallants, for us to rhyme
                I'll sweep a space, for now 'tis acting time
                We do our endeavour to please you all
                Be you ever so short or tall.
                And if you think you are so wise:
                Hold peace, our actors are in disguise;

Our play is like a troubled dream;
And all may not be as it seems.

CLACK   It is my niece, as Master Sentwell promised.

TALLBOY   Amie, Amie.

CLACK   Peace, resume your merriment.

AMIE   We are not of the ragged sort, but some of the
royal trim.
And if you don't believe me, what I say,
Step in St. George and clear the way.

(*The chant ends.* MERIEL *comes forward as St. George.*)

MERIEL   I am St. George, that noble champion bold:
That in times past did lift the Spanish gold.
'Twas I that killed the dragon with a touch:
And with my sword did smite the Drunken
Dutch.

OLDRENTS   This hero has a familiar voice.

MERIEL   But now upon all sides am I beset:
Oh, wife, come tell me, what should I do yet.

(*Enter* RACHEL *as St. George's wife.*)

RACHEL   Oh, George you are a fine hero no more:
For you are vex'd by both the rich and poor:
Parliament and King, the country and the town,
The city and the court conspire to bring you
down.
And now, when troubles fall in lots
Comes bold St. Andrew of the Scots.

(HILLIARD *comes forward as St. Andrew.*)

HILLIARD   I am St. Andrew fra' the North,
The land o' bonnie Scotland O!
Where oatmeal cakes mak' men o' worth,
And lovely spankin' lassies O!
The land o' thistles, rock an' dike,

O' hardy men and heroes O,
For Scotland's sons know how to strike
Wi' dagger and wi' claymore O.

(*St. George and St. Andrew fight.*)

MERIEL   Oh, good St. Andrew, pity me
For I am much beset,
The court, city and country
All make me moan and fret.

AMIE   See where they come.

(SPRINGLOVE *comes forward.*)

SPRINGLOVE   I am a city merchant
And Jangler is my name;
With bags of gold and bills of sale
I mean to win this game:
This game I mean to win, brave boys
And whirl the money round;
Fight, George, for my monopoly
I'll give you pound for pound.

(*The* COURTIER *comes forward.*)

COURTIER   I am a noble courtier
And Scraper is my name;
With loyal obedience to my king
I mean to win this game:
This game I mean to win brave boys
Stand, George, for our King's right;
To levy taxes as he please,
And fight whom he will fight.

(VINCENT *comes forward.*)

VINCENT   I am a country gentleman
And Scyther is my name;
My fields of sheep and corn and wheat
Will suffer in this game:
This game I mean to win brave boys
So George, come to the fight;
Defend my barns stocked high with grain
'Gainst both their armies' might.

OLDRENTS   This fellow speaks to the purpose.

HEARTY   Amen to that!

WIFE   If you three mighty subjects
                Had poor St. George at heart;
                You'd all combine together
                And take the nation's part.

MERIEL   Oh wife, thou'rt wrong in all of this
                These are no foes of mine;
                By pressing of their suits to me
                They show more love than thine.

RACHEL   Thou silly saint, oh how thou'rt wrong
                They mean to slay thee before too long.
                Of quarrel they've not had their fill,
                And now comes one who'll help them kill.

                (*The* SOLDIER *comes forward.*)

SOLDIER   I am a valiant soldier
                And Slasher is my name,
                With sword and buckle by my side
                I mean to win this game;
                This game I mean to win brave boys
                And that I will make good,
                And from your dearest bodies all
                I'll draw your trembling blood.

MERIEL   Oh! hasher Slasher, don't thou talk so hot,
                For in this room thou knows not whom thou's
                                                    got;
                We'll hop thee and chop thee as small as flies
                And send thee over the seas to make mince pies.

ALL   Mince pies hot, mince pies cold
                Mince pies in the pot nine days old.

                (MERIEL, COURTIER, SPRINGLOVE, VINCENT *and*
                HILLIARD *all fight the* SOLDIER. *Then confusion
                sets in and all fight each other.* WIFE *looks on,
                horrified. The* ACTOR *comes forward.*)

ACTOR   Accurs'd be he that first invented war!
             They knew not, ah, they knew not, simple men,
             How those were hit by pelting cannon-shot
             Stand staggering like a quivering aspen leaf
             Fearing the force of Boreas' boisterous blasts!

             (*During this, all begin to fight* MERIEL. *She is
             surrounded. The five swords lock around her
             neck. She drops her head in a posture of
             death.*)

WIFE   O naughty men, that did'st but seek your gain
             That which you coveted, you now have slain.

AMIE   But here be two to bring him from the grave:
             The Priest and Lawyer; one will surely save.

             (*The* LAWYER *comes forward.*)

LAWYER   This is as bad a case as e'er judge sat in:
             I'll bring him back to life, but all in Latin.

WIFE   He'll ne'er understand, his tongue is English.

LAWYER   Fear not: Non spirat, sed spiro: George ex
             mortuis resurge.

             (MERIEL *does not raise her head.*)

WIFE   Away lawyer, your medicine works only for
             old foreign devils.

             (*The* LAWYER *goes. The* PATRICO *comes
             forward.*)

             Now who comes here?

PATRICO   I am the priest and you should know me for I
             cost you enough.

HEARTY   I smell sedition here!

OLDRENTS   Peace, Hearty.

WIFE	Then, priest, give your blessing.
PATRICO	Arise St. George, for priest and God command That you resume your mortal life: now stand!

(*Again* MERIEL'S *head doesn't come up.*)

WIFE	Oh dismal priest, your prayers are all in vain.
PATRICO	I cannot give this man a second birth: He is alive in heav'n, but not on earth.

(*The* PATRICO *goes.* AMIE *comes forward.*)

AMIE	But see, how fair is George's skin. Methinks he was a maid after all, and now I recognise her; it is Utopia, and her life was in four seasons as we now shall hear.
CICELY	(*holding baby*) In spring she was a little child Ever meek and ever mild.
LIZ	In summer, blushing virgin maid, Never yet by man betrayed.
MEG	In autumn she gave birth to hope - A babe in shadow of the rope.
JOAN	In winter, Justice to her said: "We'll persecute you till you're dead."
HEARTY	This is not fit matter.
CLACK	(*waking*) Are they jerring of justices?
OLDRENTS	'Tis all in jest.
AMIE	So priest and lawyer, though so wise Can't cause Utopia to rise: But here comes one with little ken Who'll strive to make her live again.

(SHORT-HAIRED BEGGAR *comes on.*)

AMIE Pray tell me, fellow, in your strange bones and rags, who art thou?

SHORT-HAIRED BEGGAR I am a beggar.

AMIE But, beggar, cans't thou play the doctor and bring fair Utopia to life?

SHORT-HAIRED BEGGAR Yes master, I can be a doctor.

AMIE What diseases can'st thou cure?

SHORT-HAIRED BEGGAR Why, the hitch, the stitch, the wheezes, sneezes and all diseases. For all men and women do begin in my state of beggary and must come to it again at the last, so I am the cure for all things.

AMIE Well, beggar doctor, cure me that man.

SHORT-HAIRED BEGGAR Yes, master if I can.

(*The* SHORT-HAIRED BEGGAR *gets out a bottle.*)

Hey there, take a little of this bottle
And let it run down thy throttle.

(MERIEL *is motionless.*)

WIFE Thou silly fool, that's no cure.

SHORT-HAIRED BEGGAR No, you never knew a doctor take a short job in hand but what he made a long'n of it.
But I've got another bottle in
My pocket called Commonwealth and plain
That will bring a dead man to life again.
Here take a little of this nip nap
And let it run down thy tip tap.
Arise Utopia and live again!

(MERIEL *raises her head and comes to life.*)

WIFE   He is alive and now returns to reign!

MERIEL   Aye, but I'll no more play St. George; from
            now on I'll be Utopia.

AMIE   But who comes here?

            (RANDALL *comes on, holding a hobby horse.*)

            Faith, 'tis old Beelzebub. Hello, Bobsjack,
            pray tell me some of your rigs.

OLDRENTS   My man Randall! Has he a part with 'em?

RANDALL   They were well set to work when they made
            me a player. What is it that I must say?

AMIE   Tell me some of your rigs.

RANDALL   Ah! Now as I was going down the road, 'twixt
            Nottingham and Retford, I saw a chambermaid
            peeping through the window. She didn't beat
            the bed but she did bite the pillow. Lord I
            have never been funny in my life and am hard
            put to start now.

            Ladies and gentlemen, e'er so bold,
            To eat plum pudding before it's half cold
            My hat is dumb and cannot spake,
            Pray put something in for St. George's sake.
            With all my heart, I'm glad my part is done so
                                                    soon.

MERIEL   Let old George lie and fine Utopia stand
            Let people dwell in freedom through the land:
            And nevermore will hunger, lash and pain
            Stalk in good old England's land again.

HEARTY   For all my good nature, this sport has gone
            too far. The king is still the king and not to be
            mock'd -

CLACK   Enough of it. You pack of beggar actors, this
                 is no play, it is sedition pure and simple!
                 Take them away to be whipped.

RACHEL   Stay, for we are not beggars.

                 (MERIEL *and* RACHEL *reveal themselves*.)

                 Your sadness, father, could not suffer us
                 To live in your house so we resolved to make
                 A progress into begging, when we were
                 Informed by your good steward Springlove -

OLDRENTS   My daughters!

                 (SPRINGLOVE *comes forward*.)

SPRINGLOVE   Sir, all your sadness lay in fearing for
                 Their destiny: which they could quit
                 By making it a trick of youth and wit.
                 We struck a bargain and it was agreed
                 We'd beg to absolve your fortune, not forneed.

CLACK   But a-hey what is this? These things in rags
                 are now your daughters?

OLIVER   'Sblood, my beggar bitches!

OLDRENTS   Never was father happier to recover his own.

AMIE   And for my part, uncle do you stand so
                 pleased with my return?

CLACK   Aye. For I had thought your fortune wed away
                 to a clerk.

AMIE   I am to be wed, sir, but to no clerk.

TALLBOY   My fate revives!

AMIE   I am, as soon as it can be contriv'd, to be
                 married to this beggar.

CLACK   A beggar! Thinks't thou I'd scour the
countryside to save you from a clerk that I
may dance a jig and hurl my wig i' the air to
see you match'd to a maunder. I shall not have
it so.

SPRINGLOVE   But -

CLACK   Nay, if we all speak - as I said before. Seize
upon him.

                       (CLACK *bears down on* SPRINGLOVE. *The*
                       PATRICO *suddenly intervenes. All look at him.*)

PATRICO   Stay your hand. Let Justice silence keep,
Beggars and gentlefolk alike stay dumb
And close-tongued cleave unto Patrico's words.
Last year, as autumn 'gan to pull her cloak
Across the sun, and our crew's summer jaunt
Did falter in the face of rugged gales,
A woman in her middle years, but roughened
Past the use of forty winters, joined our crew.
So worn and hobbled by her life was she,
That on her second night within our band,
She laid her head upon a mound of straw
And spoke that strummel for her place of death.
I, striving to turn age from dark thoughts,
Sought to enliven her with foolish hopes,
Which, spurned, she did instead confess
Her sins and whole life's story. She had been
                                          fair
In gentle blood, and gesture to her beauty,
Which could not be so clouded with base
                                      clothing
But she attracted love from worthy persons,
Which (for her meanness) they express'd in
                                      pity,
For the most part. But some assaulted her
With amorous, though loose desires, which she
Had virtue to withstand. Only one gentleman
(Whether it were by her affection, or
His fate to send his blood a-begging with her
I question not) by her, in heat of youth,
Did get a son, who now must call you father.

OLDRENTS   Me?

PATRICO   You. Attend me, sir. Your bounty then
                Dispos'd your purse to her, in which, besides
                Much money (I conceive by your neglect)
                Was thrown this holy relic. Do you know it?

OLDRENTS   The Agnus Dei that my mother gave me
                Upon her deathbed! Oh the loss of it
                Was my sore grief; and now with joy it is
                Restor'd by miracle! But the woman died?

PATRICO   That very night, but press'd me to a vow
                That I would never notify her secret -

OLDRENTS   And yet you do so now and in full company -

PATRICO   - unless it were to help her son to rise
                In this harsh world, that child whom she
                Did rear through infancy, till, being unable
                To support herself, she did return him
                Whence he came; a swathed infant sleeping
                In the open air of your estate.

OLDRENTS   That child was Springlove -

PATRICO   Even so. And I
                Have kept my promise till this hour. Justice,
                This beggar whose high lineage I prove
                Makes worthy husband in both blood and love.

OLDRENTS   Most wondrous news, the best I ever heard. A
                son and three daughters gained on one
                expedition. Hear me for all then. Here are no
                beggars, no rogues, no players; but a select
                company to fill this house with mirth. These
                are my daughters; these their husbands: and
                this that shall marry your niece, a gentleman.
                I will instantly estate him in a thousand pound
                a year to entertain his wife, and to their heirs
                forever. Do you hear me now?

CLACK   A thousand pound a year?

OLDRENTS	E'en so; and the pair of them no more shall go a-begging.
CLACK	Now I do hear you. And I must hear you. And I begin to see the goodness on't. That is to say, it is a match, a marriage and a matrimony-lolly-lolly with a-hey.
TALLBOY	And must I hear it, too? Oh -
OLDRENTS	Yes, though you whine your eyes out.
HEARTY	Nephew, Martin, I will find a wife for thee.
CLACK	Nay, Clerk Martin, trouble yourself not with that, but straightway give all the beggars my free pass, without all manner of correction!
HEARTY	Methinks the justice has himself turned player.
MARTIN	I'm glad to take such tender part.
SPRINGLOVE	Good Squire, whom now I'm joyed to title Father, I have been happy, all my years, To serve you through each winter, and have only Vex'd you with my rovings i' the spring. These jaunts are past now I have found delight In Amie; and henceforward I shall prove, Now that my jovial begging course is run. Your most excellent steward and obedient son.

(SPRINGLOVE *and* OLDRENTS *embrace*.)

RACHEL	(*to* OLIVER) Are you not the gentleman that would have made beggar sport with us, two at once?
MERIEL	For twelvepence apiece, sir.
OLIVER	I hope we are all friends.
OLDRENTS	Sir Patrico, your prophecy, which was the cause of my unhappiness, I do forgive.

PATRICO	I did but relate what I saw and did not relate where I had vowed silence.
OLDRENTS	I know 'tis so. And now, Patrico, if you can quit your function and live a moderate gentleman, I'll give you and the crew a competent annuity for life.
PATRICO	I'll be withal your faithful beadsman, and spend my whole life in prayers for you and yours. So what says the crew? Shall we return straight, and spend our summer in the hospitality of good Squire Oldrents?
CONFORMIST BEGGARS	We shall. God bless the Squire.
SHORT-HAIRED BEGGAR	Not so. I am a beggar, not that I may stay forever at one rich man's gate, but that I may seek my freedom. I am for the road.
LAWYER	Aye, freedom and the road.
SOLDIER	The road is our life.
JOAN	And so say I. I have a journey still to go and no man shall prevent me.
SPRINGLOVE	Good friends, be not so hasty, stay with us but a while.
OLDRENTS	All are welcome, yet you must decide now if you are for my hospitality or no.
SHORT-HAIRED BEGGAR	Then I say no. I have tonight acted in a play which I did trust would show the thoughts that jostle in my head. But I see nothing was done, nothing shone forth and 'tis already forgot. There are those who'll never hear me; I must look for them as shall. Your play will never serve. My mystery is the road and I must be ever upon it, aye, till I can walk no further.

SOLDIER   And I too. Farewell, good friends.

MEG   And I, though I could not in words say why.

(*The* SHORT-HAIRED BEGGAR, JOAN, MEG, *the*
SOLDIER *and the* LAWYER *prepare to go, saying
their farewells to the rest of the crew.*)

RACHEL   Father, in my short begging life, which now
I trade all willingly for household comforts,
I learned to cherish all that I was born to:
Not only hearth, food, drink and quilted bed,
But all the treasures of our lives which rest
Upon the firm foundation of a home
Wrought out of love by duty and travail:
Our daily worship, music, learning and
The ties that bind us all to land and kin:
All these confer a grace upon our lives
Which marks our place betwixt the beasts and
angels.
These will I value now a hundredfold;
Nor will I jib (which was the case before)
To share these benisons with all your friends,
When your great generosity spreads
A banquet table to the wand'ring poor.

OLDRENTS   Rachel, your begging progress has brought us
more than food and drink in hand; now stretch
that hand again towards your Vincent.

VINCENT   Sir, I take her gladly and most solemnly
protest she'll never beg again.

OLDRENTS   Well spoken. How says the other sister?

MERIEL   Father, my mind is different. I feel full strong
The sweet temptation of a hearth and husband:
Yet in these three strange days, have I seen
sights
Which were but names and nothings to my past:
I bit the crust and wore the chain of poverty
And cannot easy shuffle off the marks
They pressed upon my heart; nor the delights:

> The clamour of good company and the
> midnight
> Glimmer of the springtime stars. Beyond our
> gates
> There lies a world where people fight for
> What I play'd but now; Utopia
> In England: and if a life no wisp can catch
> Of this enthused dream, then wakefulness
> Is but a wandering death. I must among them
> Lest I shrink to nothing. My journey's length
> I know not, but, like these noble beggars who do
> Brace themselves and shoulder up their load,
> I seek my freedom on the well-trod road.

OLDRENTS   Meriel, I have but regained you!

PATRICO   I do commend you, sir, to let her go. There is
              a call to the blood, and when it comes, it
              cannot be denied.

HILLIARD   Faith, Meriel, I am unprepar'd for this. Shall
              we return our steps to hunger and the
              insolence of the law?

MERIEL   Not we, good Hilliard. Our journeys now
              proceed on separate paths.

OLDRENTS   So, Patrico, your prophecy yet works on.

PATRICO   I do entreat you sir, to balance your great
              gains with this one loss.

OLDRENTS   Daughter, my blessing.

              (OLDRENTS kisses MERIEL who then says
              goodbye to RACHEL and HILLIARD.)

              I am a sage in my contentment and in
              weighing joys and sorrows, find my fortune
              plentiful.

TALLBOY   Lovers foresook should penance undergo:
              I'll join the crew to walk away my woe.

SHORT-HAIRED BEGGAR	Come, my crew. We have ten miles to travel.

[*The* BEGGARS *divide into two groups:*
RADICALS *and* COMFORT SEEKERS. *They sing
'The Beggars' Farewell', the asterisked verses
sung by one group while the other group
speaks the verse following in brackets at the
same time.*]

* RADICALS	The multitude upon the moor Shall fear no plague or cruel war When hunger's chains enslave the poor Then falls the shadow on the door.
COMFORT SEEKERS	(Take off your hats and rest your prats Let's make avail of gentry's ale So scratch your breach while others preach We'll feast and fuck and thank our luck.)
* COMFORT SEEKERS	The harman beck is at the gate But praise the Lord he comes too late Until we mock this happy fate The hanging tree will have to wait.
RADICALS	(Let firebrand youth now find the truth To spoil the feast of tithing priest Let bareshanks bold defy the cold And dunghill knaves no more be slaves.)
* RADICALS	Unto the ruffmans let's abide To roam this country far and wide We'll cut the neck of horrid pride And let our bellies be our guide.
COMFORT SEEKERS	(So damn the chills and slimy hills To hell with shires and angry squires From naught to eat, blood swollen feet We'll give our fleas a life of ease.)
*COMFORT SEEKERS	We say farewell to half our crew Who seek the light that shines anew And though our hearts be split in two God bless the paths that you pursue.

RADICALS   (So curse and steal and clean your heels
Go nip and foist and thence to roist
Though beggars breed was born to bleed
The magic stars will mend our scars.)

ALL   Now go in peace the die is spun
For journeys ended and begun
And may the Lord who sends the sun
Be with you till your road is run.

(OLDRENTS *and his household and the* COMFORT
SEEKERS *go off one way. The* RADICAL BEGGARS
*gather at the door leading to the outside
world. The light fades.* SPRINGLOVE *remains
with* AMIE. SPRINGLOVE *looks out wistfully at
the departing beggars.*)

SPRINGLOVE   May the new crew walk together well: and
                         the old
Crew rest their feet and find good lodging in
Familiar straw.

(AMIE *goes to* SPRINGLOVE *and takes his hand.*)

             Shall we walk to the rest, Amie?
Freedom long has been my heart's dear goal
And now I find it in another soul.

(*They follow* OLDRENTS' *party. The* RADICAL
BEGGARS *open the door to the outside world. A
beautiful England of green foliage and blue
sky awaits them.*)

* RADICALS   Come vagabonds it's time to go
Must face our elemental foe
These acorns form a crooked row
Sweet chance allow one tree to grow.

COMFORT   (No more the whip nor jailor's grip
SEEKERS   No more to roam from happy home
No more to starve we've pigs to carve
No more to say we've done the day.)

(*The* RADICAL BEGGARS *go. The birds sing.
Slow fade to blackout.*)

THE JOVIAL CREW: OVERTURE

BORN to the LIFE

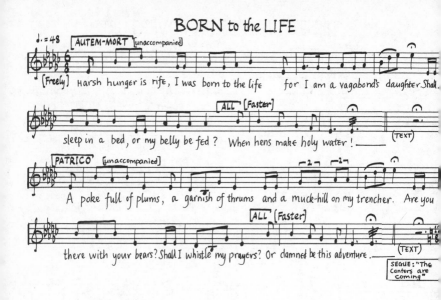

AUTEM-MORT [unaccompanied]

♩.=48

[Freely] Harsh hunger is rife, I was born to the life for I am a vagabond's daughter. Shall

ALL [Faster]

sleep in a bed, or my belly be fed? When hens make holy water! _____ (TEXT)

PATRICO [unaccompanied]

A poke full of plums, a garnish of thrums and a muck-hill on my trencher. Are you

ALL [Faster]

there with your bears? Shall I whistle my prayers? Or damned be this adventure. _____ (TEXT)

SEGUE: "The Canters are Coming"

BORN to the LIFE [Reprise]

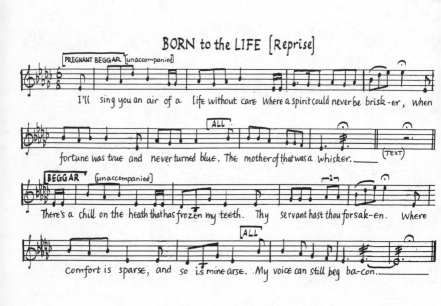

PREGNANT BEGGAR [unaccompanied]

I'll sing you an air of a life without care Where a spirit could never be brisk-er, When

ALL

fortune was true and never turned blue. The mother of that was a whisker. _____ (TEXT)

BEGGAR [unaccompanied]

There's a chill on the heath that has frozen my teeth. Thy servant hast thou forsak-en. Where

ALL

comfort is sparse, and so is mine arse. My voice can still beg ba-con. _____

THE CANTERS ARE COMING

So! Throw a good scruff to the singers and dancers ___ Throw a good scruff.... etc.

Rufflers, runagates priggers and prancers ___ Throw us white money whenever we ask it ___ Rufflers runagates...etc.

Throw us white money....etc... } Doxies, dells and bawdy baskets ___ {

Trouble ye not thy bodkin stranger ___ Our entertainments hold no danger

Trouble ye not ....etc ___ our

entertainments....etc ___ Go shoe the goose and saddle the sow ___ Go shoe the goose and saddle the sow } The

Canters are coming among you now. ___ { The

REPEAT with words of the 3rd and 4th quatrains taking the 2nd time bar

Well-versed in the whids of the ruffian's art. ___ Well-versed in the whids of the ruffian's art } GIP! quoth Gilbert when his

mare doth fart. "Pthth"

FRUMMAGEM RUMMAGEM

♩ = 80

[violin]

[Freely] SOLO: Pretty child with fifteen fathers, each as wild as any
Live through fifteen summers, while the win-ter snow may

1st

other; Pretty child, pray would you rather Wapping mort was not your
clean you? Will Old Nick and fif-teen drummers take you

2nd [violin]

mother? Will you from me ere I wean you?_____

♩ = 100 A Tempo [SPOKEN] [ALL]

[Drums]

Frummagem rummagem cackle and crow, beggar is born and

[SOLO]

beggar is bred. Frummagem rummagem let him grow then hang him all ex-cept his head. [I'm

[ALL] [SOLO] [ALL] [SOLO] [ALL] [SOLO]

youth] 'tis fair [I'll fly] to where? [The highest steeple I can find. I'll steal] take care [your

[ALL] [SOLO]

REPEAT TWICE MORE
with words of 2nd & 3rd verses

eyes] you dare [while clever hands will rob you blind.]

[ALL]

Frummagem rummagem gabble and croak, he'll face an army with his fist. Frummagem rummag

take his oak, then hang him up and let him twist. Frummagemma rummagemma

frummagemma rummagemma frummagemma rummagemma rum, rum, rum.

THE MERRY GRIG (Dance)

BING AWAST

(1) **GIRLS:** Take by the shank and give it a what? **BOYS:** Take by the shank and give it a wank. **GIRLS:** The
(2) **BOYS:** Lads at their peak with pizzles of teak? **GIRLS:** Lads at their peak with pizzles of teak. **BOYS:** Cry

cardinal's hat! well pray fancy that.
higgledy piggle! Their vowing to niggle.

[Instrumental]

Dal $

ALL: In this jovi-al crew we're to

hell and be damned, with our certainties few and too hastily crammed. With a phrase of the canting we're

EIGHT TIMES

armed for the fray: Bing a-wast! In Come a-ranting! Let's up and away. Bing a-wast! Come a-ranting! Let's

up and away. Bing a-wast!

DONEGAL

♩. = 50

BONES / **BASS DRUM**

𝄋 mf C — F — C — C

Fresh mist on the morning and tears on my eyes, Take me back to the dawning of
My life in that country's a lifetime away, Take me back to the mountains of

G — C — sub PP — F — C — G — C — F

Donegal skies.
Ballybofey ⟶ Where the wanderer's welcome is kindest of all. Take me back to my darling, my
TEXT [DURING MUSIC] "MOVE ONWARD...." etc - - - - - -

G — C (clarinet)

Dal 𝄋 for 2nd and 3rd verses
(go to CODA during 3rd time)

sweet Donegal.

CODA C — F — G — C — C — F — G — C (clarinet)

{ Take me back to my darling, My sweet Donegal. Take me back to my darling, My sweet Donegal.
[+TEXT]

NIENTE

MUMMERS' CHANT

FRUMMAGEN RUMMAGEN [Reprise]: CURTAIN CALL

Frummagem rummagem fiddle and fuck, beggar may live or beggar may aie. Frummagem rummagem pluck this duck, then hang him up and see him fly. [Our tale] is told [Yet still] un-folds [of beggars lost and beggars found Who'll face] the cold [needs must] be bold [The world is turning upside down.] Frummagem rummagem babble and moan, The devil take this merry gang.. Frummagem rummagem break their bones and watch them dancing when they're hanged. Frummagemma rummagemma frummagemma rummagemma frummagemma rummagemma rum, rum, rum.